THE ART & CRAFT OF
STONESCAPING

THE ART & CRAFT OF
STONESCAPING

SETTING & STACKING STONE

DAVID REED

Lark Books
A Division of Sterling Publishing Co., Inc.
New York

To Celia

∽

Editor: Chris Rich
Art director: Celia Naranjo
Principal photographer: Evan Bracken (Light Reflections, Hendersonville, NC)
Illustrator: Scott Lowery
Editorial assistant: Evans Carter
Production assistants: Bobby Gold, Hannes Charen

The Library of Congress has cataloged the hardcover edition as follows:
Reed, David, 1957–
    The art & craft of stonescaping : setting & stacking stone /
  by David Reed.
      p. cm.
    Includes index.
    ISBN 1-57990-018-2
    1. Stone in landscape gardening. I. Title.
  SB475.5.R44 1998   97–49856
  624.1'832—dc21   CIP
                                  AC

10 9 8 7 6 5 4 3 2 1

Published by Lark Books, A Division of
Sterling Publishing Co., Inc.
387 Park Avenue South, New York, N.Y. 10016

First Paperback Edition 2007
© 2000, by David Reed

Distributed in Canada by Sterling Publishing, c/o Canadian Manda Group, 165 Dufferin Street, Toronto, Ontario, Canada M6K 3H6

Distributed in the United Kingdom by GMC Distribution Services, Castle Place, 166 High Street, Lewes, East Sussex, England BN7 1XU

Distributed in Australia by Capricorn Link (Australia) Pty Ltd., P.O. Box 704, Windsor, NSW 2756 Australia

If you have questions or comments about this book, please contact:
Lark Books, 67 Broadway, Asheville, NC 28801, (828) 253-0467

Manufactured in China

ISBN 13: 978-1-57990-018-2 (hardcover) 978-1-60059-130-3 (paperback)
ISBN 10: 1-57990-018-6 (hardcover) 1-60059-130-2 (paperback)

For information about custom editions, special sales, premium and corporate purchases, please contact Sterling Special Sales Department at 800-805-5489 or specialsales@sterlingpub.com.

Cover photo: Terraced walls built by Art Garst
Pages 6-7 (left to right): Anasazi dwelling, first century A.D., southwestern U.S.; dry-laid stone steps, North Carolina Aboretum of Asheville; dry-stacked terraced walls, Waynesville, NC

TABLE OF CONTENTS

INTRODUCTION

Think stone. The sun-warmed, rough surface of a rock in your hand; snow-dusted boulders on a hillside. Magnificent Incan temples; abandoned campfires, ringed with blackened rocks. Glistening pebbles in a creek bed; stacked stone walls on a terraced Italian hillside. The megaliths at Stonehenge; the stepping-stone path to your garden. Our fascination with stone—its permanence and simplicity, its beauty and mystery—is as old and enduring as stone itself.

Dry-stacking and dry-laying stone (building without mortar) is more popular today than ever. Why? In our high-tech world, stonescaping allows us the rare opportunity to reconnect with our natural surroundings. What's more, working with stone offers tangible, deeply satisfying, and lasting rewards. Walking past a stone structure you've built yourself is a pleasure like no other. Set three stones to make a garden bench or stack a small retaining wall—just a few feet long and a couple of feet high—and you'll know exactly what I mean.

Stonescaping without mortar is surprisingly easy. All you need to start are rocks, gravel, a few basic tools, and this book. You don't have to be a male with arms of steel, a wealthy landowner with a huge estate, or an engineer with hundreds of specialized tools. If you can handle a shovel, wield a hammer, and lift small stones; if you can find a few square feet to call your own; and if you're eager to spend some time outdoors now and then, the world of stonescaping is yours.

The chapters that follow will walk you through every basic step of dry-stacking and dry-laying stone. After you've read the chapters on tools and materials, just select a project that interests you, read the instructions, and begin. No matter what you make—a tranquil waterfall, a paved walkway, a flight of formal stone steps—the results will be enjoyed for generations to come.

CHAPTER ONE

TOOLS AND EQUIPMENT

T he tools and equipment used for dry-laid and dry-stacked stonework are remarkably simple compared with those of most crafts or building trades. They're usually quiet, inexpensive, and low-maintenance items, too. Browse through this chapter, take inventory of what you already own, and then set aside some time for visiting flea markets and hardware stores.

DON'T BE INTIMIDATED by the number of tools described in this chapter! You certainly don't need them all in order to build attractive stone projects. Start with the tools listed below and add others as you find them.

I look for most of my stoneworking tools at the local flea market. In fact, I'd guess that half the tools I own were bought used. (I think of these purchases as a form of recycling.) When I can't find what I need at the flea market, I visit a hardware store or one of the home-improvement warehouses. If you choose the flea-market approach, plan on making numerous trips; you can never be sure of finding exactly what you need on any given day. A good hardware store, on the other hand, will order any tools that aren't in stock.

BASIC TOOLS

- Wheelbarrow
- Shovel
- Mattock
- Stonemason's hammer
- Brick-and-block mason's hammer
- Steel rebar, 2 feet (61 cm) long
- Cold chisel, 8 inches (20 cm) long
- Level (the longer, the better)
- Several five-gallon (19 liter) buckets
- Heavy-duty leather gloves
- Safety glasses

WHEELED IMPLEMENTS

A good wheelbarrow, either metal or plastic, is a must for moving stones. The standard barrow (or pan) sizes are 4 and 6 cubic feet (.11 and .17 m³). I prefer the larger models; because they carry more, I don't have to make as many trips with whatever I'm hauling.

This nurseryman's hand truck is one of the larger models.

Garden carts are stable and good for moving small loads of stone.

Even when these larger models are empty, however, they're noticeably heavier than smaller ones, and metal barrows are a good bit heavier than plastic versions. A metal barrow does have one big advantage: It will withstand plenty of abuse.

For moving large paving stones and the large, flat stones that cap off dry-stacked walls, a barrow will work, but a hand truck or dolly makes the job easier. A smaller version of the nurseryman's hand truck shown on the opposite page will work just fine, as will a sturdy garden cart. My neighbor Jackie Taylor says she prefers moving stones in a cart because a cart is more stable than any wheelbarrow.

No matter what type of barrow, cart, or hand truck you choose, it should have large pneumatic tires. On uneven ground, these work better than small solid wheels.

Shovel with round blade and turning spade

Shovels with square blades

DIGGING TOOLS

Three kinds of shovels come in handy for grading sites and scooping gravel: one with a square blade, one with a round blade, and a turning spade.

A shovel with a square blade is most efficient for leveling rough spots and scooping up gravel. A shovel with a round blade works for general soil-digging purposes. A turning spade—the stout shovel commonly used by gardeners—has a flat, rectangular blade with a squared-off end and a strong forged metal socket for a wooden or plastic handle. I use this spade for digging at odd angles and in tight spaces, prying rocks out of the ground, cutting out roots, and adjusting the positions of paving stones.

The mattock is similar to a miner's pickaxe, but instead of having two opposing narrow picks, it has a slightly curved digging blade at one end and a small, wedge-shaped blade at the other. This tool is useful for loosening packed earth, adjusting the positions of paving stones, loosening embedded rocks from the ground, and cutting out roots.

Mattock

Another tool in the digging category is the pry bar, also known as a digging bar or shale bar. This

Pry bar

solid piece of steel is about 1¼ inches (3 cm) in diameter at its pointed end and tapers to about ¾ inch (2 cm) in diameter at its other end. It's most useful for adjusting the positions of large stones and for prying stones out of the ground. Any pry bar that doesn't bend easily is a good one. Mine, purchased at a flea market ten years ago, is 5 feet (1.5 m) long, weighs about 35 pounds (16 kg), and is still as straight as can be. Similar versions are available at many hardware stores.

Crowbars, which are similar to pry bars but smaller and lighter, make effective stone-prying tools. They range from 2 to 3 feet (61 to 91 cm) in length. One end of the tool is flat and slightly flared; the other end is curved in a "J" shape.

HAMMERS AND SLEDGES

Professional stonemasons use many kinds of hammers to break and split stone, including sledge hammers, mashing hammers, stonemason's hammers, blacksmith's forging hammers, striking hammers, and brick-and-block mason's hammers. Of the dozen or so hammers that I currently own, I have two favorites. One is a 2½-pound (1.1 kg) blacksmith's

Stonemason's hammer

forging hammer. The other is a 3-pound (1.4 kg) stonemason's hammer.

The lighter hammers work well for trimming small protrusions and sharp edges from stones. Medium-weight hammers work well for driving chisels when you need to trim or split off larger sections. Heavy hammers, such as sledges weighing 4 pounds (1.8 kg) or more, are best for making smaller stones out of big ones.

Sledge hammers, with their heavy, rectangular heads, come in different weights. For most stone projects, a 10-pound (4.5 kg) sledge is as heavy a model as you'll ever need, although a 16-pound (7.3 kg) sledge may be necessary to break up very thick stones or concrete. My 5-pound (2.3 kg) model, with its 2-foot-long (61 cm) hickory handle, sees a

10-pound (4.5 kg) and 5-pound (2.3 kg) sledge hammers

lot more use than any of my heavier sledges.

A mashing hammer, which is a short-handled sledge, comes in 2-, 3-, and 4-pound (.9, 1.4, and 1.8 kg) weights. Its head has two wide, flat surfaces that work well for striking chisels and breaking stones, and its short handle allows for good control. The 2- and 3-pound weights are best for general use.

The stonemason's hammer comes in 3-, 4-, and 6-pound (1.4, 1.8, and 2.7 kg) weights and is best for tasks that

Mashing hammer

require a lot of force, such as removing large sections from stones or breaking thick rocks. The head is narrow and flat at one end and tapers to a wedge shape at the other. A 3-pound mason's hammer is a good choice for breaking and trimming stone.

Blacksmith's forging hammers come in a variety of weights. The ones I usually see at the flea market weigh 2 to 3 pounds. Although this hammer is made

Brick-and-block mason's hammers (left); blacksmith's forging hammers (right)

for forging metal, the wedge shape at one end of its head makes it exceptionally useful for chipping and trimming stones. The other end, which is square and flat, works well for striking chisels.

The brick-and-block mason's hammer, which is useful for working on smaller, thinner stones, weighs 1 to 1½ pounds (.5 to .7 kg). One end of the head looks like the head of a carpenter's framing hammer. The other end consists of a tapered blade, which can serve as a chisel when you're splitting a stone or trimming its thinner edges.

A 3-pound rubber mallet is useful for setting flagstone and other paving materials such as concrete slabs, bricks, and faux stones. Its rubber head won't chip or scratch stone surfaces. This tool can also be used to make minor adjustments to the stones in a dry-stacked wall.

Rubber mallet

MEASURING TOOLS

A tape measure is handy for measuring stones as you select them to fit, determining the heights of stone benches and walls, and measuring paving sites. Rock dust and grit are hard on these tools, so wipe the entire tape off with a damp rag now and then. Heavier-gauge versions, with 1-inch-wide (2.5 cm) tapes, last much longer than narrow, flimsier tapes. A 25-foot-long (7.6 m) self-retracting metal tape will cover almost all stoneworking situations.

For measuring a stone's thickness or the space to be filled by a stone, a folding rule works in place of

STONE SLEDS

I once had the good fortune to witness the use of a stone-moving implement from days gone by. I was traveling along a picturesque mountain road, when I came around a bend and was forced to a complete stop. Before my eyes was a sight that made me feel as if I'd stepped back in time. Crossing the road was a farmer, with his two large draft horses harnessed to a 10-foot-long (3.1 m) stone sled (or stone boat) loaded with about 2 tons (2034 kg) of fieldstone.

The sled's stout timber runners were 6 inches by 6 inches (15 by 15 cm) and had wide steel strips attached to their bottoms. The platform itself was only 8 inches (20 cm) off the ground, so stones could be tumbled onto and off of it easily, with much less effort than it takes to load a pickup or flatbed truck. As I watched, I realized what gathering stone must have been like before the invention of the combustion engine. The stones in the 150-year-old dry-stacked chimney shown here were probably transported in this manner. 🏋

This dry-stacked stone chimney, constructed more than a century ago, is as sound today as it was when it was built.

a measuring tape. This device is made up of a series of narrow wooden sections, which extend when unfolded to 6 feet (1.8 m) in length. A folding rule can also serve as an adjustable template when you're searching for a particular stone to fit next to others.

You'll need at least one level. The high-quality versions are made of wood or metal; less expensive models are made of plastic. A 9-inch-long (23 cm) torpedo (or plumber's) level, or any level up to 2 feet (61 cm) in length, is handy for adjusting individual stones within a paving project. The 2-foot-long models are also useful when you're setting steps. For gauging the level and pitch of several stones in a paving project, a 4- or 6-foot (1.2 or 1.8 m) level works best.

A straight 8- to 10-foot-long (8.3 to 3.1 m) 2 x 4 or similar piece of lumber, without any bends or bows, is helpful as you work on paving projects. Setting its narrow edge down on your pavers will help you locate dips between the upper surfaces of stones that don't meet evenly.

When you want to trim or break stones in order to create faces and corners, a carpenter's square is also handy for marking straight lines.

CUTTING TOOLS

Chisels are used for scoring, splitting, cutting, and chipping stone. Although a hammer will work alone to split or break stone, using the correct chisel gives you more control. For striking a chisel, a 2- to 3-pound (.9 to 1.4 kg) blacksmith's forging hammer or a mashing hammer works best.

The most useful chisels for stonework are cold chisels, 8 to 10 inches (20 to 25 cm) long, with shafts about ¾ inch (2 cm) in diameter and blades ranging from 1 to 3 inches wide (2.5 to 7.6 cm). (Note that the end of the blade of a cold chisel is beveled on both surfaces.) Longer cold chisels are available, but they're harder to control when you

strike them with a hammer. Carbide-tipped chisels are best. If you're a professional stonemason, their hefty price is worth paying because the carbide tips last 20 times longer than regular steel.

Three other helpful chisels are brick chisels, pointed chisels, and pitching chisels. A brick chisel's cutting edge, which ranges from 2½ to 3½ inches (6 to 9 cm) in width, works well for scoring lines across stones and for breaking away unwanted sections. The pointed chisel is the best kind for breaking off small protrusions from stone faces. The pitching chisel, which is similar to a carpenter's chisel in that only one surface of its cutting edge is beveled, is used to shear off larger unwanted lumps from stone surfaces.

A double-insulated electrical circular saw, rated at 13 amps or more, with a 7¼-inch-diameter (18 cm) abrasive blade, is useful for scoring flagstone before you break it. The abrasive blades are made of a composite material that works on masonry and metal surfaces, as well as on stone.

A masonry cut-off saw, with a blade 12 or 14 inches (30 or 36 cm) in diameter, will cut stone and

Brick chisel (left); three cold chisels (right)

Carbide-tipped chisels

galvanized culvert pipe. These saws are similar to chain saws but make use of large abrasive disks instead of chains. They weigh close to 30 pounds (13.6 kg), so they're not for everyone! If you'd like to try one out, many rental stores carry them.

TOOLS FOR SPREADING AND SEATING GRAVEL

Dry-stacked retaining walls and many paving projects are seated on beds of gravel. A sturdy garden rake with rigid steel teeth will not only help spread the gravel, but will also help grade the site (the teeth will remove small stones and larger debris from the soil). In addition, a rake is useful for cleaning up your work area; it will remove any rock chips you've generated while breaking or splitting stones.

Five-gallon (19 liter) buckets, available at home-improvement centers, are invaluable for hauling gravel, collecting smaller stones, storing hammers and smaller tools, and—when they're turned upside down—sitting on when you need a break.

The gravel base under a paving project, as well as the backfill between a stone retaining wall and the soil bank behind it, must be thoroughly settled by poking it with a metal rod. A number of tools will work for this purpose, including tire irons (I prefer these because their extra thickness at one end makes them easy to grasp); 2-foot-long (61 cm) sections of rebar, which are available at home-improvement stores; and lengths of steel rod. A dull point at the working end of any setting tool improves its performance.

For spreading rock dust or sand under paving stones, either a mason's trowel or a stucco trowel is helpful. I find that the rectangular stucco trowel is easier to control. A hand broom is useful in paving

Top to bottom: two tire irons, a section of rebar, and a steel rod

and wall projects when you need to sweep up stray bits of sand, rock dust, and gravel.

For some paving projects, you must tamp down a layer of rock dust on top of a gravel bed. An 8-inch by 8-inch (20 by 20 cm) metal plate tamper, available from masonry suppliers, is the tool of choice, but a homemade tamper is easy to construct. Just nail a solid, 8-inch-square piece of thick wood to one end of a 5-foot-long (1.5 m) 4 x 4. To add handles, attach 2 x 2s to opposing sides of the 4 x 4, setting each one at a workable angle.

Stucco trowel, used to spread out a layer of rock dust beneath paving stones

BENCH GRINDER

The edges of hammers, the cutting edges of chisels, and the edges of digging implements will all round off with use, so regular sharpening is a must. I use an electric bench grinder with a ⅓-horsepower motor and two wheels, each 6 inches (15 cm) in diameter and ¾ inch (2 cm) wide. If you don't want to buy a grinder, take your tools to a professional sharpening service.

A "COME-ALONG"

The "come along"—a small, portable, hand-operated winch—helps move very large stones. The model I use has a cable drum and is rated to pull 1½ tons (1525 kg), which is plenty of pulling power. Heavier-duty models, made to pull or lift 3 to 5 tons (3051 to 5085 kg), are also available. These larger models incorporate chains or heavy-duty cables. When using come-alongs, keep an assortment of chains, webbing straps, and ropes on hand.

Heavy-duty come-alongs, one with chains and one with cable

RAMPS

Pieces of 2 x 10 lumber, 4 to 8 feet (1.2 to 2.4 m) long, make good ramps when you need to move large stones into a truck bed or set capstones on a wall.

Also, keep a few short logs on hand. As you'll learn in chapter 3, these can serve as "wheels" for rolling large flat stones from one place to another.

LANDSCAPE FABRIC

Dan Snow, a dry-wall builder in Vermont, where winters are harsh, always covers the soil banks behind his retaining walls with landscape fabric, which is available at most nurseries and home-improvement warehouses. This protective layer prevents frost-heaved soil from passing through the gravel backfill and out through the face of the wall.

SAFETY EQUIPMENT

Safety goggles—the kind that make you look like you're ready to go scuba diving—are uncomfortable and fog up too much for my taste. I discovered a lightweight pair of safety glasses that offer full protection by wrapping around the sides of my head, and that provide good ventilation. When I'm working, I keep these glasses dangling from a strap around my neck, ready to be worn at any time.

Wear tough leather gloves when you work with stone. Make sure they fit well; loose gloves won't let you get a good grip on stones or tools. For good foot support and protection, wear a pair of thick leather boots. When you're working on a paving project, good knee pads will save wear and tear on your trousers—and on your knees.

CHAPTER TWO

STONE AND GRAVEL

*T*he kind of stone you'll use for your project will depend on the kind of project it
is, the stone available in your area, and
whether you plan to collect the stone from the land
or purchase it from a stone yard. In this chapter,
you'll learn a bit about the kinds of stone that are
best suited for dry-stacked and dry-laid projects,
how to estimate the amounts of stone and gravel
you'll need, where to find these materials, and how
to get them to your building site.

BEFORE YOU TACKLE YOUR FIRST PROJECT and purchase or gather stone for it, you'll need to familiarize yourself with some of the vocabulary that stonemasons use.

THE MASON'S LANGUAGE

■ The *face* of a stone is the surface that is exposed when the stone is set in a retaining wall or paving project. Some stones have one or more obvious faces; others may need some trimming or splitting to create one.

■ *Rubble stones* are irregularly shaped stones without obvious faces and can range from fist-sized to the size of a half-gallon (1.9 liter) milk jug. These stones make useful additions to the gravel backfill between a dry-stacked retaining wall and the soil

The backfill behind this dry-stacked retaining wall is made up of rubble and pea gravel.

bank behind it, so save all the rubble that turns up during your gardening and landscaping endeavors. Crushed aluminum cans and chunks of broken concrete block can also serve as rubble.

■ *Rough-quarried stone* is stone that has been removed from large veins in the earth, either by blasting the veins with dynamite or by drilling and prying the stone away, removing it layer by layer. These stones (common types include flagstone, sandstone, granite, and limestone) vary in shape and size, but if you handpick your stone at a stone yard, you'll find good rough-quarried stones for dry-stacked walls and paving.

■ *Fieldstones* are stones found loose on the ground or embedded in the soil. Weathered fieldstones lend a rustic look to any stone structure, and like some quarried stones, if they're selected carefully, they're often suitable for dry-stacked projects and for use as stepping stones or pavers.

■ *Road bond* (also known as *ABC* or *crusher run*) is a mixture of crushed stone and rock dust that is used in some paving projects.

■ When you pave with flagstone, you must set the stone on a bed of gravel topped with a layer of either *rock dust* (pulverized crushed rock) or *coarse* (not fine) *sand*. Fine-tuning the position of each paving stone is much easier when the paver rests on material less coarse than gravel. To fill the joints between paving stones, some masons use rock dust or sand in combination with gravel.

■ For most dry-stacked stone work and paving projects, you'll need *washed crushed stone*, also known as *gravel* and sometimes incorrectly called *pea gravel*. (Pea gravel is dredged from rivers and, unlike crushed stone, is rounded and smooth.) Note that when I use the word "gravel" in this book, I'm referring to ⅜-inch to ½-inch (9 to 12 mm) crushed stone.

Although you may use pea gravel instead of crushed stone, the latter is usually easier to find in bulk quantities. In addition to helping set the stones in your wall, crushed stone provides excellent drainage within and behind stone retaining walls, and prevents water from building up behind them.

■ *Backfill* is the mixture of gravel and optional rubble that is used to fill the space between retaining-wall stones and the soil bank behind them.

■ *Courses* are the horizontal layers of stones in any dry-stacked project.

■ A *joint* is the space between any two stones in a stone structure. Every stone wall has joints between its courses, and every course has joints between the stones in it. A *running joint* occurs when the joints in a series of courses fall along the same vertical line. Avoid creating these, as they weaken stone structures.

Avoid running joints such as those shown in the wall above. They may weaken a wall and will detract from its appearance.

■ *Stretchers* are stones with long horizontal faces. They're laid on top of smaller stones in the course beneath in order to "break" several joints with one stone.

■ *Capstones* or *coping stones*, are the uppermost stones on a wall. They should always be the largest and heaviest stones you have on hand, with as much surface area as possible. A workable size for a capstone is about 2 feet (61 cm) long, 2

feet wide, and 2 to 4 inches (5 to 10 cm) thick. The largest capstone I've ever placed was an abandoned piece of granite curbstone, 8 feet (2.4 m) long, 18 inches (46 cm) wide, and 4 inches thick. I was thankful for the help of three friends.

■ Dry-stacked retaining walls slope slightly backward. This slope or lean is known as the wall's *batter* and serves to increase the stones' force of gravity against the soil bank. For retaining walls 2 to 5 feet (61 to 152 cm) in height, a standard batter of 5 to 10 degrees works well.

■ In cold, wet regions, moisture-laden soil can freeze to a depth of 2 to 3 feet (61 to 91 cm). When it does, it swells and heaves upward—a process known as *frost heaving*. Shifting soil behind and beneath dry-stacked walls can be a problem, as its movement can shift the wall upward and outward. Using gravel beneath the first course of a wall and in your backfill material will help prevent frost heaving by allowing water to drain away before it can freeze. Covering the exposed soil bank with landscape fabric will help keep loose soil from pushing through the gravel and out through the joints between stones.

■ *Shim stones* are small, thin, flat pieces of stone that are used to adjust the overall height of larger stones. Because they show in the finished wall, they should have attractive faces. You may either look for them at a stone yard or make them by using a hammer and chisel to split layers from sedimentary stones.

■ *Anchors* (or *deadmen*) are long stones that are set randomly into retaining walls, with their lengths positioned across, rather than along, the length of the wall. Because their back ends extend into the

Strategically placed small stones help prevent gravel backfill from escaping through wide joints in the wall.

gravel backfill, these stones "anchor" the wall, adding to its structural stability.

- *Chinking stones* are small stones or pieces of stone that are used to fill in gaps in wide joints between larger stones.
- *Wedges* are small, tapered bits of stone used to level larger stones, either from front to back or from side to side. Whenever you trim stones, save the broken-off pieces, especially tapered ones, to serve as wedges.

SUITABLE KINDS OF STONE

The three main types of rock are igneous, sedimentary, and metamorphic. Igneous rock (basalt and granite, for example) is extremely dense and hard. Sedimentary rock is often colored by iron deposits and tends to be layered. (For this reason, sedimentary rock such as medium-density sandstone is especially easy to split.) Metamorphic rock includes any kind of stone that has been transformed by heat, pressure, or chemical action into another type of stone. Limestone, for example, can metamor-

phose into marble.

Within these three general categories are many kinds of rock, some of which are better than others for dry-stacked and dry-laid stonework. Stones that are soft and that crumble at their edges (soft sandstones and schist, for example) aren't the best. Structures built with these and other soft stones will sometimes survive in hot, arid climates. In temperate climates, however, the combination of consistent moisture and freezing weather causes soft stones to disintegrate quite quickly.

Schist—a banded, layered, very porous rock—doesn't wear well in paving projects and can't handle the weight of a wall. Individual pieces of schist make fine landscape highlights, but do select the largest, thickest pieces you can find; they won't disintegrate as quickly as smaller pieces. Also avoid stones with a very high iron content. Oxidized iron, released by rain, will cause unsightly streaking.

The chart on the next page provides descriptions of suitable stones.

STONE	WEIGHT RELATIVE TO SIZE	COLOR	GRAIN	WORKABILITY	STRENGTH
Basalt	Heavy	Grey to black, and brown	Fine	Moderate	Excellent
Gneiss	Medium	Grey to black, with bands of white quartz	Medium	Good	Good
Granite	Heavy	Pale grey to pale red	Medium to coarse	Difficult	Excellent
Limestone	Heavy	Pale green, grey, tan, white, black	Even	Moderate	Good to excellent
Sandstone (dense)	Medium	Grey to brown	Even grain	Good	Good to excellent
Slate	Medium	Black, blue, dark grey	Fine	Good	Good for paving

STONE YARDS AND OTHER SUPPLIERS

The best way to find out what types of stone are available in your area is to visit a stone yard. The people who own or run these yards are almost always friendly and helpful, although they may not have time to spare when they're busy loading orders or sending out their own crew of stonemasons. Late mornings and early afternoons tend to be their slowest times.

Stone yard and quarry operators can always identify the stone they sell, of course. If you can't tell one kind of stone from another and you're gathering stone from the land, test the stone by striking it with a hammer. Use as much force as you'd use if you were trying to crack it. If it flakes easily or crumbles, move on in your search. Alternatively, you can collect a few samples and take them to a stone yard or to the geology department at your local college or university and ask for some help identifying them.

A good stone yard will offer a wide variety of stone.

Loose piles of fieldstone at a stone yard

Unless you have the time and energy to collect stone from the land, you'll probably need to purchase building stone from a stone yard or quarry. If there's a quarry nearby and you're able to haul the stone yourself, the quarry may be an option, but I go to stone yards because they're often more conveniently located, approachable, and likely to make small deliveries. Quarries, which supply stone yards and gravel dealers, usually sell in very large quantities, their equipment is huge, and the big dump trucks moving about their sites can be a bit intimidating. I've parked my pickup truck next to a small mountain of gravel at a quarry and watched the gravel being loaded by a machine with a bucket large enough to scoop up the truck itself.

Suppliers of stone, gravel, and road bond are usually listed in the phone book under "Stone," "Gravel," or "Sand and gravel."

HOW STONE IS SOLD

At a typical stone yard, you'll find huge piles of quarried stone and fieldstone; large boulders; and pre-selected stones arranged on pallets and either contained in wire baskets or wrapped in plastic.

Stone is usually sold by the ton or portions thereof. Prices vary from one kind of stone to another, of course. Fieldstone, for example, is more costly than most rough-quarried stone because gathering it is so labor-intensive. The price per ton rises when the stones have been pre-selected and placed in wire baskets on pallets. You'll also pay more if you want to handpick your own stones, one by one, from the loose piles. I think the extra cost of handpicking is worth it, even when it takes me a couple of hours to select a few tons of stone.

Pre-selected quarried stone stacked on pallets at a stone yard

STONES FOR DRY-STACKED WALLS

Whether you're handpicking stone at a stone yard or gathering it on the land, keep in mind that the overall shape of each stone will determine how well the stone will stack. Stones with at least two flat, opposing surfaces and block-shaped stones with squared edges that will fit together tightly are the best. Don't discount stones with protrusions or irregular edges. If the protrusions can be chipped or split away easily in order to make the surfaces more uniform, the stones will work fine.

A wall made with block-like stones of different shapes and sizes is visually captivating, although filling in around the stones in each course can be a bit challenging. Stacking one course on top of another is easier with thinner stones.

Don't forget to gather some shim stones—smaller, flat stones ranging from the size of a paperback book to the size of a cassette tape cover. You'll use them to make up for height differences when you've stacked two stones of different sizes side by side. Collecting shim stones in five-gallon (19 liter) buckets makes them easy to transport.

CAPSTONES

A secure and easy way to cap a dry-stacked retaining wall is to use stones with large, even surfaces and uniform thicknesses of 2 to 5 inches (5 to 13 cm). Stones this size also make good pavers, steps, and benches.

Thin fieldstones lend a rustic, layered look to a retaining wall.

Unfortunately, it may take some searching and a few visits to stone yards to accumulate enough capstones for a wall. Although you won't usually find sections labeled "Capstones" at stone yards, some stone suppliers offer—at a premium price—large, pre-selected slabs suitable for use as pavers, capstones, and benches. With a little effort, I've always been able to find comparable stones in the yard's loose piles.

Don't let a lack of these large stones stop you from beginning your wall. Instead, start building the wall and keep your eyes peeled for capstones every time you visit the stone yard. When your wall is 8 inches (20 cm) short of its finished height, stop stacking stones. This will leave enough room to set capstones as you find them and, if your capstones vary in thickness, to fill in any spaces beneath them.

An elegant retaining wall built with block-shaped stones

FIELDSTONE PAVERS

Unlike a wall stone, which must have two flat surfaces, a fieldstone paver only needs to have one good surface. As you select a paver, you must consider its surface area, thickness, and weight.

Thick, heavy pavers with surface areas of at least 2 feet (61 cm) square are difficult to move, but their weight makes them more stable than smaller stones. If you want to work with large stones, select ones that are 2 to 6 inches (5 to 15 cm) thick.

Small pavers are easier to move, but if they're too thin, they'll shift. To avoid this problem, make sure that any small pavers you select are very thick, so you can set them well down into the gravel. An

8-inch by 8-inch (20 by 20 cm) paver, for example, should be at least 6 inches thick. Small pavers often provide an easy and attractive way to fill voids between larger stones.

Whether your pavers are large or small, their edges should be squared and flat rather than tapered. Why? Because setting the thin, tapered edge of one stone next to another stone creates a small hollow that will trip the first person who steps into it. Trim any pavers with tapered edges so that once they're set with other pavers, the overall paved surface will have as few dips in it as possible. You may set untrimmed tapered pavers along the outer rim of a paved area or in a stepping-stone project.

Small stones used to fill gaps between large pavers must be thick, or they'll shift. The ones shown above extend 6 inches (15 cm) down into the gravel bed.

Three tips: When you're selecting pavers, avoid stones such as cut marble, the smooth surfaces of which get slick when they're wet; stones with obvious cracks in them; and schist, which can't withstand the wear that paving stones get.

FLAGSTONE PAVERS

A flagstone paver works best when it's at least 1½ feet (46 cm) square and 1½ to 3 inches (4 to 8 cm) thick. Thinner flagstones will hold up in mortared paving projects, but not in dry-laid ones. And remember: The smaller the stone, the thicker it should be. Large flagstones should be around 1½ to 2 inches (4 to 5 cm) thick; smaller flagstones should be about 3 inches thick.

ESTIMATING REQUIRED QUANTITIES

How many tons of stone you'll need for a dry-stacked wall or dry-laid paving project will depend on what you're making, how tightly you fit the stones together as you stack or lay them out, and the weight and density of the kind of stone you plan to use. If you're a beginner, read this section carefully, and know the dimensions of the project you plan to build before you visit the stone yard.

As a rule of thumb, dry-stacked projects such as retaining walls require about 1 ton (1017 kg) of stone for each 30 to 35 square feet (2.8 to 3.3 m²). This dimension includes the face of the wall and its upper surface. If, for example, your wall is 15 feet (4.6 m) long, 2 feet (.6 m) tall, and 1 foot (31 cm) wide, you'll need stone for (15 x 2) + (15 x 1) square feet—or 45 square feet (4.2 m²). One-and one-half tons (1525 kg) of stone should be enough for this hypothetical wall.

Before purchasing fieldstone pavers, determine the square footage of the paving site. The amount of stone you'll need will vary, depending on what kind it is and how thick the pavers are, but if their average thickness is 4 to 6 inches (10 to 15 cm), buy about 1 ton for each 40 to 50 square feet (3.7 to 4.6 m²).

For dry-laid flagstone paving projects, about 1 ton of stone will cover 75 square feet (7 m²).

Purchasing an extra ¼ ton (254 kg) of stone for every 2 tons (2034 kg) you think you'll need will not only save you extra trips to the stone yard, but will also allow you to pick the best stones as you build. Just stack any leftover stones (or culls) in a corner of your yard until you're ready to tackle another project or until a friend or neighbor, inspired by your efforts, wants to do some stonescaping of his or her own.

Gravel, unlike stone, is sold by the cubic yard. The amount required to fill the space behind a retaining wall will vary widely, depending on how much rubble you include in the backfill mix and

This driveway was covered with gravel rolled into asphalt. Bands of colored stone were added to complement the various colors of the gravel.

on the average thickness of your wall, but using the following formula will provide a rough estimate. The formula is based on two assumptions: that the average width of the backfill area is about 1 foot (31 cm), and that you won't include much rubble. (If you have rubble handy, by all means use it; you won't need to use as much gravel.)

(Wall height x wall length x 1 foot) ÷ 27 = Cubic yards of backfill

If your wall is 20 feet (6.1 m) long and 2 feet (.6 m) tall, for example, the backfill area will be approximately 20 x 2 x 1, or 40 cubic feet (1.12 m³). To convert cubic feet to cubic yards, divide the number of cubic feet by 27. In our example, 40 divided by 27 is roughly 1½ cubic yards.

The stones used in most paving projects are set on a gravel bed that is usually about 4 inches or .3 feet (10 cm) thick. To estimate an amount of gravel for this bed, use the following formula:

(Site length x site width x .3) ÷ 27 = Cubic yards of gravel

As an example, if your paving site is 20 feet long and 2 feet wide, the gravel bed will be 20 x 2 x .3 or 12 cubic feet (.34 m³), which is roughly one-half of a cubic yard. If your project isn't rectangular or square, use estimated averages for length and width.

TRANSPORTING STONE AND GRAVEL

Stone yards will arrange for delivery, and if you need more than 1 ton (1017 kg) of stone, paying the extra cost is worthwhile. If you're making a small project or just want to pick up a few stones to naturalize an area, it's well worth picking up the stone yourself.

Two cautionary notes: When the ground has been soaked by rain, a heavy vehicle loaded with stone will leave deep tire tracks on your lawn. Wait until the ground is dry and firm. Also, if you have a buried septic tank on your property, don't drive over it!

If the stone yard has pallets and a forklift available (many do), the best way to handpick and transport larger stones is to arrange the stones on a pallet as you choose them. When you're finished picking, the forklift operator will transfer the pallet to a large scale, where the stone will be weighed. Then the operator will lift the pallet into the bed of your truck. A standard ½-ton (508 kg) pickup will safely transport 1500 pounds (681 kg)—enough stone for a good day's work on any stone project!

If you plan to handpick and haul the stone yourself, consider the following tips:

- Before hauling heavy loads, add a few extra pounds of air to the rear tires on your truck.
- Stone yards usually have plenty of pallets, but you may want to check first to make sure you can have one. Also make sure the pallet will fit into the bed of your truck.
- While you're selecting the stones, arrange them carefully on the pallet, placing the larger stones around the edges and filling in the center with smaller stones. This arrangement, which helps stabilize the stones on the pallet, will make the fork-lift operator's job—and your own driving—safer.

After you've handpicked stones and arranged them on a pallet, a forklift transfers the pallet into the bed of your truck.

Almost any kind of vehicle can haul small amounts of gravel. A half-dozen five-gallon (19 liter) buckets will fit into a car. When I work at sites to which vehicles don't have access, I fit about 20 of these buckets into the bed of a small pickup truck. Four buckets will fit into a large wheelbarrow, which can go just about anywhere.

FINDING STONE

Gathering your own stone from the land offers a sense of accomplishment that going to stone yards just doesn't provide. Locating accessible stone sources, however, requires extra time, and moving the stones can be physically demanding.

In the workshops I give on dry-stacking, one or two people always exclaim that their land is nothing but rock. The thought of buying stone seems unreasonable to these folks. Even if you know of land that seems loaded with free stone, however, think carefully about whether you really want to gather it. If the stone is easily accessible, go right ahead. If the land is very steep or the stone is still embedded in the soil, think twice!

There's no way around the fact that carrying stones by hand over rough terrain and transporting stones in a wheelbarrow is hard work. Beginners tend to forget that even a half-filled garden cart or wheelbarrow is heavy. Trying to negotiate a steep hillside with a cart or barrow full of stone can also be unsafe. If you'd like to try gathering your own stone anyway, some useful tips follow:

- Find out who owns the land. Although a pile of stones may look abandoned, someone may have plans for it.

Abandoned stone structures are good sources for stone, but many have historical value. Always ask for permission before taking stone from someone else's property.

- The cold months of the year are the best for stone searches. When vegetation has died back, it's much easier to see what's on the ground. In addition, the only snakes you're likely to encounter are ones in hibernation. (If you should discover any hibernating creatures, cover them back up and continue your gathering a few feet away. Critters living in the wild have enough trouble as it is with development and other disturbances created by humans.)
- Sometimes, where wooded areas meet more open ground, you'll find fieldstones that were left in piles when the land was cleared. In some parts of the world, especially in the British Isles and the New England states, these stones were com-

monly used to build stone fences. In the Southern Appalachian mountains where I live, I often see piles of stone left through the years as fields were cleared for crops and livestock. When I've rummaged through these piles, I've found good building stone mixed in with a lot of rubble.

- The foundations and chimneys of old houses were often built with a combination of stones, mud, and chinking stones. If you happen upon ruins such as these, consider disassembling them; they can yield great building stone. Just don't forget to get permission from whoever owns the land. For historical, aesthetic, and sentimental reasons, some people would prefer that these old structures remain undisturbed.

RECYCLING GOOD STONE

Several years ago, I disassembled what remained of the mortared stone steps and foundation of a building across the road from the house where I live. This building had been abandoned long ago; nothing was left of its main wooden structure. I was able to remove some of the stones by hand; others took a little persuasion from a pry bar. I also used a small crow bar and a 3-pound (1.4 kg) mason's hammer to chip away lingering pieces of mortar.

As soon as I'd gathered enough stone to lay out the first course, I started building a dry-stacked retaining wall in front of an earthen bank that I'd cut into a slope. When I needed more stone, I'd return to the site and retrieve another load. Now, not more than 400 feet (122 m) from the building site, there stands a finished wall built with recycled stone.

A retaining wall built with "recycled" stone

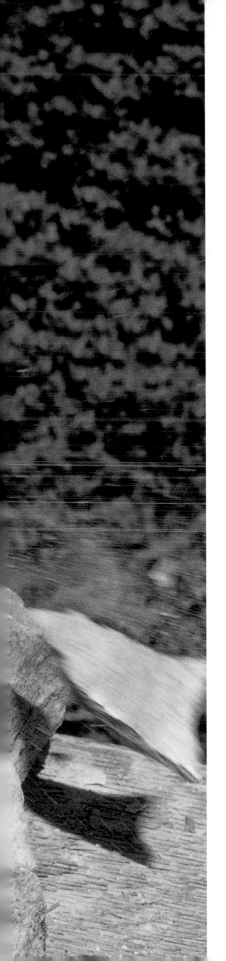

CHAPTER THREE

WORKING WITH INDIVIDUAL STONES

*W*hen working on any dry-stacked or dry-laid project, you're bound to face situations in which you can't seem to find the right stone for a perfect fit. Learning to trim and split stone by breaking it across and along the grain will save you both time and money. You'll save time by creating the perfect stone instead of having to search for it, and you'll save money by not having to order huge quantities of stone in the hope that somewhere in the pile you've ordered, the perfect stone awaits.

*The following section, written by a professional mason and friend of mine, will help
you learn how to trim a stone in order to create a face.*

TRIMMING STONES FOR WALLS

by Robbie Oates

During my evolution as a stonemason, I've almost completely changed the way in which I work with stone. When I first started, I used only gathered stones with natural faces and corners. Now I build walls almost exclusively with stones that I have delivered from a stone yard and then trim.

The philosophical "mission statement" with which I started has evolved into a more practical viewpoint, largely because finding good face and corner stones was getting more and more difficult. In my area of the country, sources for good rock had been picked through, and turning to stone companies for help wasn't a solution. I couldn't count on getting good faces and corners unless I overordered by 35 percent and then culled out the undesireables. I had two choices at this point: I could give up on my progress towards a super-tight style or learn how to create faces and corners on the stones to which I had access.

Learning to trim and split stone requires only a basic understanding of the structure of stone, some practice, and a few essential tools: hammers, chisels, and a square. You'll also need safety glasses, heavy-duty gloves, and a sturdy work table.

The type of rock you've selected will determine to a large degree the final shape of the stone. Rocks with consistent crystalline structures, such as granite, sandstone, limestone, and some quartzite, can be split as well as trimmed. These tend to be the easiest rocks to work with.

Rocks that have horizontal layers and/or inconsistent crystalline structures are more difficult to trim because the vibration created by striking the stone with a hammer often causes the stone to split along the grain rather than breaking cleanly across the grain. Many types of quartzite, gneiss, and schist fall into this category. When you trim a rock in this category, you can only remove small amounts of material, so take the time to select rocks that already come as close as possible to matching the shapes you want.

The purpose of trimming a wall stone isn't necessarily to flatten its face. Your goal is to make the stone meet surrounding stones as tightly as possible. In the example offered here, the stone is first trimmed to create four edges (where the face of the stone and its four adjacent surfaces meet) that all rest on the same vertical plane. Then one end of the stone is also trimmed so that the stone can be placed at one end of a wall, where two of its adjacent faces will be visible.

The rock shown in the following photos is a dense sandstone from Virginia and was purchased at a stone yard. It was a very workable rock, easy to trim and to split.

Imagine that one long edge of your work table represents the face of your wall and that the surface of the table represents a course of stone in the wall. Select a "blank" (the stone you'd like to trim) and position it on the table as if you were setting it into the wall.

Next, pull the blank out slightly so that its face overlaps the long edge of the table. Now imagine a vertical plane rising from the table edge and slicing through the overlapping stone. Your goal is to trim the stone so that the four edges around its face all rest on this plane.

Using your square as a straightedge and a 3-inch-wide (8 cm) chisel as a marker, trace a line across the top of the stone. This line should rest right over the edge of the table top.

Now mark the ends of the stone in the same fashion, placing one edge of the square on the table top and aligning the other edge with the edge of the table. Also mark the bottom of the stone.

Step back to check the traced lines. They should all align with the imaginary plane rising from the long edge of the table.

The next step is to create a preliminary fracture in the rock's crystalline structure. You won't actually break the rock at this stage, but the fracture will make the rock much easier to trim when you're ready. Position a 3-inch-wide chisel on the traced line and strike it, using moderate force, with a hammer. Repeat, moving the chisel along the lines on all four sides of the rock.

I use a carbide-tipped chisel to deepen the fracture, working my way around the lines once again.

Next comes trimming. Working your way around the lines, strike the chisel much harder than you did to create the fracture. Your goal is to remove shards of rock along the traced lines. Work along the top and bottom surfaces first.

To trim each end, position the rock with the end facing up. To keep the rock stable, be sure to prop it up firmly with other rocks.

Finally, trim away any ragged edges.

With a bit of practice, you'll soon be able to turn out a well-trimmed face.

If you'd like to make a corner stone to place at the end of the wall, repeat these steps to trim one end of the stone. Position your square as shown at left so that your traced lines (and the face you're about to trim) will be perpendicular to the face you've already trimmed.

The stone shown underneath the chisels is a fully trimmed corner stone.

TRIMMING FLAGSTONE PAVERS

Because flagstone is sedimentary and tends to separate along its layers, trimming it across the grain requires a special technique.

First define the portion to be removed by using a straightedge and chisel to score a line across the face of the stone. Prop the stone up at a tilt, with the marked line at the lower end. Position a hose with a nozzle at the top of the stone so that you can direct a slow, steady stream of water down the stone and across the scored line. Put on your safety glasses and ear plugs.

Next, using a double-insulated circular saw with an abrasive blade, you must cut a straight, shallow groove, ¼ inch (6 mm) deep, along the scored line. Position the front edge of the baseplate on top of the stone, with the saw's guide mark over the scored line. Hold the saw at an angle so the blade doesn't touch the stone. Turn the saw on, carefully lower the spinning blade down until it touches the start of the scored line, and guide the saw gently back and forth. Don't exert any downward pressure on the blade; instead, allow the weight of the saw to do the cutting. If you need to lift the blade guard in order to keep track of the cut, do so, but be extremely careful! The water flowing over the stone will reduce dust in the air as well as wear on the blade.

Two important warnings here: Make absolutely sure that your circular saw is double-insulated before you run water anywhere near it. Also, if you've plugged the saw into an extension cord, waterproof the joint where the cord and the saw plug meet by wrapping it tightly with duct tape.

Now set the stone on the gravel bed of your paving site, with the scored side facing up. To raise the stone slightly, position a section of 2 x 4 underneath the portion of the stone you want to save, aligning one edge of the board with the groove in the stone. Keep as much of the stone as possible in contact with the gravel; this will help the stone absorb the shock when you strike it with a hammer. The portion of the stone you want to remove should now be raised above the gravel bed.

Using a 2- to 3-pound (.9 to 1.4 kg) hammer, strike the portion of the stone you wish to remove. If this portion is especially long, use two hammers simultaneously, holding one in each hand. In most cases, the stone will break cleanly along the groove. If only one layer breaks off, score, cut, and break off the remaining material.

Using a circular saw to score a flagstone paver

MAKING SMALL STONES FROM BIG ONES

Whether you're working with pavers or wall stones, a single blow from a sledge hammer can transform a large fieldstone into two smaller stones. I often find that the surfaces created by the break make excellent faces on wall stones.

Using a 5-pound (2.3 kg) sledge to break a fieldstone across the grain

SPLITTING STONES

In order to create a smooth face on a rock, you may need to split away an uneven layer. The veins (or layers) in sedimentary rock are often visible.

Position your chisel between two veins and strike the chisel with a hammer. Then move the chisel along the vein and strike it again. Repeat, striking at different points along the vein, until the layer splits off.

MOVING STONES

Because you set stones one at a time, you may not realize right away just how much weight you're moving around—a ton (1017 kg) or more for a retaining wall! After a few hours, however, you'll feel the effects. The tips below will help you expend less energy and protect you from injuries, too.

- To prepare yourself for the strenuous physical activity ahead, start each stonework session by stretching and warming up. If you're new to this kind of work, be careful to pace yourself. Start with short sessions, small projects, and relatively small stones, and build up your strength over time.
- When you bend down to pick up a stone and when you lift it up, always bend at the knees, not at the waist.
- Pay attention to what you're doing. On several occasions, I've had a large stone roll in an unintended direction and have found myself dancing something like an Irish jig while trying to get out of its way.
- If you have a come-along, by all means use it for moving large stones. First, to help the stone slide along more easily, try to pry it up and slip one or two boards underneath it. Next, hook the tool to a heavy object that will remain stationary: a large tree, a car, or a truck will do. Attach the chain, rope, or webbing to the stone and to the come-along.

Then crank the tool's lever handle, while a friend uses a pry bar to guide the stone as it slides along the boards towards the object to which the tool is fastened.

■ To move large, relatively flat stones, roll them on several 2-foot-long (61 cm) logs, each 4 to 8 inches (10 to 20 cm) in diameter. Smaller diameter pipes will also work, but only on hard, even ground.

■ A pry bar tied to a stone and used as a lever reduces the force required to move a stone.

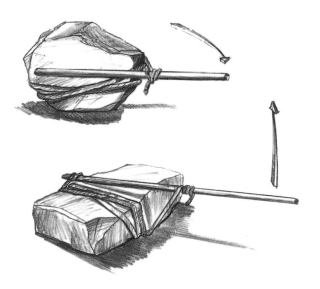

■ Some large stones can be walked up ramps by turning the stones end for end.

■ To move very large stones, first turn a wheelbarrow on edge, right next to the stone. Push the stone into the wheelbarrow. Then lift the stone up onto its end and move around to the other side.

Pull the wheelbarrow and stone towards

you until the wheelbarrow is upright.

CHAPTER FOUR

DRY-STACKED RETAINING WALLS

*W*ell-built, dry-stacked retaining walls
will survive the test of time, the forces
of nature, and a good deal of human
activity. The method used to build these beautiful
walls is simple, and most of the steps are similar to
the ones used to dry-stack other stone structures.

THE THEORY

The primary purpose of a retaining wall is to retain a bank of soil behind it. Unless the wall is constructed properly, it won't do its job, so before you begin this project, I'll introduce you to the basics of dry-stacked wall construction. As you read this information, refer to the cross section of the finished retaining wall shown on the opposite page.

Backfill

A dry-stacked retaining wall is built several inches away from the bank it's meant to retain. This distance will vary, depending on the sizes of the stones you set in the wall. When you set a large stone—perhaps 18 inches (46 cm) in depth—you'll leave about 4 inches (10 cm) between its back end and the soil bank. Some of the largest stones that make up the wall's face may be deep enough to extend all the way back to the bank. A stone 6 inches (15 cm) deep, set in the same course, might have an 18-inch (46 cm) space behind it. As you work, you'll fill these spaces with gravel and, if you have any, rubble stones.

Wall Height

The easiest dry-stacked walls to build are generally 2 feet (61 cm) or less in height. These low walls work well for retaining existing low banks of soil or banks cut into sloped areas, but they're sometimes built simply to highlight one portion of a landscape. The photo on page 49 shows a good example.

A level wall retains the gravel bed in front of this southwestern home.

Any cut into an earthen bank leaves the exposed soil vulnerable to wind, rain, and frost heaving, and invites the soil to shift. The larger the exposed area, the stouter the retaining wall must be.

Although it's possible to dry-stack retaining walls 5 feet (1.5 m) or taller, you must build them with much larger stones, make them thicker, and increase their batter to 15 degrees. You must also set the stones in the wall's first course slightly farther away from the bank in order to accommodate the wall's extra thickness. Unless you have access to extremely large stones, avoid dry-stacking walls more than 5 feet in height.

Wall Thickness

The thickness of a dry-stacked retaining wall will vary depending on the sizes of the stones in it and the finished height of the wall. Walls up to 2 feet in height should be about 12 to 20 inches (31 to 51 cm) thick, while walls between 2 and 5 feet tall should be 20 to 24 inches (51 to 61 cm) thick.

Batter

Dry-stacked retaining walls are always battered slightly; they lean backwards in order to prevent shifting soil in the bank from moving the stones forward and toppling the wall over. If you're building a tall wall and don't care for the look of a severe degree of batter, consider making a series of shorter terraced walls, one above the other. (Tips on building terraced walls are provided in chapter 8.) An alternative is a vertical mortared wall, consisting of concrete blocks filled with rebar and concrete, set on a concrete footer, and faced with stucco or stone.

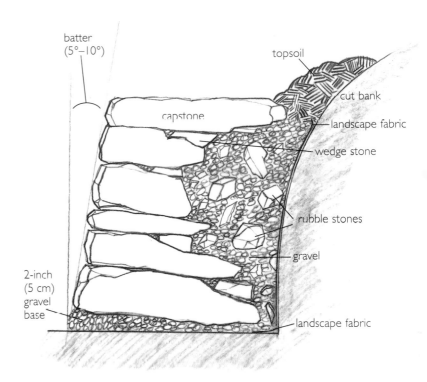

A retaining wall 5 feet (1.5 m) or more in height should be built with very large stones. This wall, in the northwestern United States, was stacked with basalt stones.

Stone-Setting Angles

Stones in a dry-stacked retaining wall should be set with their upper surfaces level or pitched slightly toward the back of the wall. This helps maintain the wall's batter and the thrust of the stones against the soil bank.

Upper Surfaces

The illustrations and photographs on the opposite page offer three methods for finishing off the top of

a wall. If the bank behind your wall is the same height from one end to the other, the wall should be the same height along its entire length so that it follows the line of the bank. The level surface provided by the capstones can serve as a perfect site for potted plants or, if the height is right, as a bench.

If the soil bank tapers downward at one end, the wall should do the same. One way to taper a wall is to construct it in "steps" by capping it off at varying heights. To build this type of wall, you'll start at the lowest end of the bank, setting two or three courses of stone from one end of the bank to the other. Then, starting at the low end again, you'll start setting capstones. When you reach the point at which the soil bank rises above the last capstone you've set, you'll stop setting capstones and stack another course or two of stone along the remaining length of the wall. Then you'll set more capstones until the wall needs to step up again, and continue by repeating these steps until the wall is finished.

Another way to construct a tapered wall is to taper the capstones so that they follow the upper surface of the bank itself. The graceful incline created by the sloped capstones offers a beautiful visual effect, but if the taper is a steep one, you won't be able to use the wall as a bench.

Wall Ends

The stacked ends of a level retaining wall or the tall end of a stepped wall may butt up against another structure such as the foundation of a home. Wall ends may also be freestanding, but keep in mind that freestanding ends are vulnerable, especially if they extend into high-traffic areas. A passing garden

The retaining wall to the left, with its stepped upper surface, consists of a concrete foundation and a block wall faced with mortared quarried stone. This style is known as the "dry-stacked look."

A low, level wall with wide capstones makes a good place to sit.

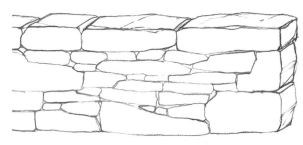

Level retaining wall with squared corners

A "stepped" retaining wall in progress

A "stepped" wall, made by setting capstones at different levels, rises to meet the bank behind it.

This wall tapers down with the bank behind it.

A tapered wall is created by reducing its height from one end to the other.

cart or climbing children can wreak havoc on their structure, so be especially careful to fit the end stones well.

On any retaining wall, freestanding ends must have stone "corners" in order to retain the backfill between the wall and the soil bank. Corners can be

built in a number of ways. One common method is to combine two types of stones: block-shaped, chunky stones and a few longer tie stones that run all the way from the front face

of the wall to the soil bank. Remember that these tie stones, as well as any other stones that will show at the front of the wall and around the corner, must have two adjacent faces.

Another way to construct a corner is to position a single, large, very thick stone on end, at a 90-degree angle to the face of the wall.

The level gravel driveway in this setting made an ideal work area for wall building.

BUILDING A DRY-STACKED RETAINING WALL

FOR SEVERAL YEARS, I've led stone workshops in my home state. The one that we photographed for this book took place at the North Carolina Arboretum at Asheville. Of the dozen people who registered for this course, only one had any previous wall-building experience, but we only needed two, separate 8-hour-long workshops to complete this 60-foot-long (18.3 m) wall.

The wall-building instructions you're about to read and the photos that accompany them will walk you through every step we took in the workshop. By the time you've finished this chapter, you'll be ready to build your own dry-stacked retaining wall.

Planning

As in any building project, a little bit of planning and organizing will make your work easier. Before beginning your wall (or any stone project), visualize or sketch the finished structure in its surrounding landscape. You'll need to decide how thick the wall will be, whether it will be straight or curved, and whether it will taper down to the ground or stand squared and level.

The characteristics of your site will play a large role in determining the decisions you make. The workshop retaining wall shown below is 2 feet (61 cm) tall; its height was determined by the cut in

The wall built during the workshop was low enough to serve as a bench, so we added some backrest stones.

By importing soil and encircling it with a low retaining wall, stonemason Frederica Lashley created a planting bed on a level lawn.

the bank behind it. Because this wall is low, it is only 20 inches (51 cm) thick. We used stones up to 18 inches (46 cm) deep. The gravel backfill behind the stone was an average of 2 to 4 inches (5 to 10 cm) deep.

Selecting and Preparing the Site

Part of a dry-stacked wall's beauty rests in its simplicity; it requires neither mortar nor a concrete footer. It does require, however, a specific site: a mound or bank of soil to retain.

Your land may have an existing bank, a natural berm, or a berm left over from the excavation of your home site. If it doesn't, you'll need to create a berm by importing soil.

Whether you're working with an existing bank or with one you've created, the next step is to make a cut in the soil bank. In order to expedite the workshop, I arranged to have a small loader make the initial cut in our bank. The workshop members then refined the cut by hand, using mattocks and shovels to remove roots and rubble as they worked. Don't worry if you can't afford to use heavy equipment; the initial cut for a low wall can almost always be made by hand. If your soil isn't hard and compact, you can even do this without using a mattock. A shovel works well on looser soils.

As you make the cut, be sure that it angles slightly backwards to match the batter of the future wall. Loaders and other pieces of heavy equipment tend to make vertical cuts, so you must take this step even if the major work has already been done for you.

Save about one-quarter of the soil you remove (especially if it's good top soil), placing it just beyond one end of the wall site. When you've finished stacking the wall, you may need this soil to dress out the area between the capstones and the

A small loader made the initial cut for this wall. The workshop members then raked soil from the bank's upper surface to fill a few low spots and tamped it down. Exposed roots and rubble stones were removed with shovels and mattocks.

top of the bank. Make a pile of any rubble stones you encounter, too; you'll add them to the gravel backfill.

After you've cut the bank, clean away all debris from the area where the wall will be placed. This surface should be even and free of rubble. Also clear a work area 4 to 6 feet (1.2 to 1.8 m) wide along the length of your site for your tools, piles of large stone, and gravel. Your materials should be as close at hand as possible. Remove any extra soil, adding it to the soil you removed from the cut bank. Like your desk at work or your kitchen counter, the neater you keep this area, the more efficient your labor will be. If you take regular breaks to clean it up, most of the rubble and rock chips you generate will end up mixed into the backfill.

Before you begin building the wall, you may want to cover the cut bank with landscape fabric (see page 17).

Sorting the Stones

After preparing a site, I like to sort my stones by size and sometimes even by shape. Spending the time to do this familiarizes me with the stones I have on hand. I don't remember every one of them, of course, but handling them seems to leave an impression on my subconscious. When I'm building a wall, I often find myself able to locate the perfect stone from the sorted piles.

Pay attention to the shapes and faces of the stones as you sort them and leave the most obvious face of each stone facing up. This way, you'll be able to see it when you scan the pile for a certain shape or size. Save the largest, flattest stones in a separate pile; you'll use them as capstones.

Gathering Tools and Materials

Along with your piles of stones, make sure you have a pile of gravel off to one side or waiting in five-gallon (19 liter) buckets. You may also want to have several buckets filled with small shim and wedge stones.

Bring out your tools and equipment. Except for items that will rust, everything in a dry-stacked stone project can stay just where it is when you take breaks. The wind isn't likely to blow anything away, and rain won't hurt your materials either. Your project will stay pretty much the way you left it, even if you neglect it for months.

Laying Out the Gravel Bed

For a 2-foot-tall (61 cm) wall, spread out a 2-inch-thick (5 cm) layer of gravel, extending it from the cut bank to a line about 2 inches beyond where the front face of the wall will rest. If you were building a wall 4 feet (1.2 m) tall, with larger stones, you'd need to increase the width of this base by about 4 to 6 inches (10 to 15 cm). At this stage, the width of the gravel bed isn't critical; you can always increase it as you lay out the first course of stone. Use a steel-toothed rake to help spread the gravel evenly.

Setting the First Course of Stone

The first course of stone will carry the weight of the wall. To spread that weight out evenly, select stones with large surface areas. "Large" is a relative term, of course, and will depend on the sizes of the stones available to you.

Set the first stone at one end of the wall site, placing its front edge where you'd like the face of the wall to be. The stone's upper surface should slope slightly down from front to back. Pitching the upper surface of a stone towards the front of the wall, in a direction opposite to the direction of the wall's batter, makes laying the next course more difficult.

Setting the first stone on the gravel bed

Remember that unless the end of your wall butts up against a building foundation, every stone at either end serves as a corner stone, so it must have two adjacent faces—one that appears at the front of the wall and one that appears around the corner. If this stone doesn't reach all the way back to the soil bank behind it, you must fill the gap by setting another stone directly behind the first one in order to prevent the gravel backfill from filtering out from behind the wall. (Refer to the section entitled "Wall Ends" on pages 44-46 for descriptions of corner-building methods.)

Continue by setting more first-course stones, one by one, working from one end of the wall and stopping a few feet from the other end. Fit the stones as close to each other as possible. (The back ends of the stones don't need to meet perfectly, as any gaps will be filled with gravel, but make every effort to match their front ends well.)

To adjust the stones' angles, add or remove gravel or wedge stones. If points or protrusions keep a particular stone from fitting well with the stone next to it, use a stonemason's hammer and a chisel to trim the stone for a better fit.

Continuing the first course and adjusting a stone's position by pushing gravel underneath it

This first course is a good place to use stones with one large, flat surface and an opposing surface that is rounded and/or irregular. Position the rounded, irregular surfaces down into the gravel. If necessary, you may even dig down below the gravel and into the soil, in order to set the stones securely and at the desired height.

Now finish the first course by working from the unfinished end of the wall towards the stones you've already set. Why work backwards when

Add small stones to make up for the difference in stone thicknesses.

you're setting these last few feet of stone? Because if you continue forward, especially when you're building a wall that butts up against a solid structure, you'll find yourself struggling to find just the right stone for the very last space, which is often a visual focal point. It's easier to find that last stone first, and then work backwards.

If this end of your wall is freestanding, remember that the last stone in every course will serve as a corner stone.

The stones in the first course don't have to be the same thickness. To make the upper surface of the first course even along its length, just add shim stones or smaller stones on top of the shorter ones you've already set. When you've finished, stand at one end and check the overall appearance of this course to make sure that the stones are where you want them to be.

Spreading and Setting the Gravel Backfill

If you have rubble stones, scatter some of them in the void behind the first course. Then spread gravel over them and into any gaps around the back edges of the first-course stones. Now you must set the gravel around the sides and backs of the wall stones in order to level and lock them in place. (The mortar in a mortared wall locks the stones in a similar fashion.) Gravel setting is a tedious job, but it strengthens a wall considerably.

I use a piece of rebar, with one rounded end, as a setting tool. A short crowbar or the long, tapered end of a mason's hammer will also work well. Jab the tool into the gravel around the backs and sides of the wall stones, forcing the gravel into the voids. If, as you do this, the gravel disappears into a void beneath a stone, add more gravel or pull some forward from the backfilled area and continue setting it until the void is filled.

Initial setting of the gravel backfill, using the tapered end of a mason's hammer

Before setting the next course, brush back any gravel remaining on top of the first-course stones; the first few inches of the top surface of every stone should be bare. Gravel on these upper front surfaces will prevent the stones in the next course from making good contact.

Dry-Stacking the Remaining Courses

To complete the remaining courses, you'll repeat the very same steps: laying the stones in each course and then adding and setting the gravel-and-rubble backfill. As you work, keep the following tips in mind:

■ Pay attention to the wall's batter as you work. After setting every couple of courses, stand at one end of the wall, so that you're looking down its length. The slope of the wall should be 5 to 10 degrees. (If you're not very familiar with degrees, look at a clock set at 12:01. The minute

SOIL AS BACKFILL MATERIAL

I've seen many dry-stacked retaining walls back-filled only with soil, including this 100-year-old wall across the creek from my home. Most of these walls were built with very large stones and include smaller stones only when they're necessary to secure the larger ones. The mass and weight of the stones in these walls are what hold them in place. I still recommend backfilling with gravel, even if you live in an area where frost heaving doesn't occur. Gravel not only adds stability to dry-stacked walls, but due to its consistency, is also easier to manipulate than soil when you're trying to adjust the positions of the stones. ■■

When filling large voids with gravel, I sometimes use the handle of my hammer before setting the gravel with a length of rebar.

Setting gravel behind the capstones with a tire iron

hand will rest at a 6-degree angle in relation to the hour hand. The batter of your wall should look very much the same.)

■ Remember to complete the last few feet of each course by setting the corner or end stone first and then working backwards, towards the stones you've already set.

■ The key to building a fine wall is ensuring small joints by getting the surfaces of each stone to make as much contact as possible with the surfaces of the stones around it. Take your time choosing stones. When a stone looks like it will fit well in a particular spot, place it there. Sometimes, flipping the stone, end over end, may make it fit even better. If necessary, trim away small protrusions or thin tapering edges to make stones fit more tightly.

■ On occasion, you'll need to add a wedge stone to stabilize a larger stone, or a thin shim stone to adjust its overall height.

■ Always keep the next course in mind as you lay the one beneath it. If a stone has major protrusions that will present problems when you lay the next course, trim them before placing the stone in the wall.

Splitting away protruding layers of stone, bit by bit, to create a smooth surface

A curved upper wall creates a backrest for the wall beneath it.

■ Always try to break the joints of the previous course. That is, position your stones to cover the joints between the stones in the course beneath. The rule of thumb here is "two-stones-over-one, one-over-two, two-over-one," and so on. Sometimes, when particular stones fit together exceptionally well, I skip this rule of thumb, but not often and never for more than two courses. If the joints break in the same places, course after course, you'll end up with running joints—vertical spaces running through more than a single course. These create potential weak areas in the wall, as well as being visually obvious. Adding a stretcher is one way to break several joints with a single stone.

■ Because the final course of your wall—the capstone course—will bring your wall to its finished height, you'll need to do a few quick calculations in order to decide how many courses of stone to set before capping the wall off. The next section explains how.

Laying the Capstones

Setting the capstones is the final phase of dry-stacked wall construction. Start by measuring the thickness of the thickest capstone you have on hand. If that thickness is 6 inches (15 cm), for example, and you want your wall to be 2 feet (61 cm) tall, you'll need to start the capstone course when the stacked courses beneath are no more than 18 inches (46 cm) tall.

Well-laid capstones prevent the stones underneath from loosening, thus ensuring a long life for your wall. Placing the capstones just right can be a bit challenging, but the results are well worth the effort. Start by setting out a few capstones on the

Adjusting the wall height to prepare for the next capstone

ground in front of the wall and moving them around until you find a sequence that works. (The capstone layout you create on the ground may not work as well on the wall, but working on the ground is a good starting point.) Your goals are to make sure these stones sit securely on the ones

Trimming a protrusion from the edge of a capstone will reduce the gap between capstones and ensure a tighter fit.

beneath them and to match their edges as closely as possible.

Position the capstones on the wall one at a time, just as you positioned the stones in the other courses, angling the top of each one slightly backwards. To bring each capstone to the desired height, you may need to adjust the course beneath by adding stones.

Making a Bench Backrest

If you want your wall to serve as a bench, consider adding a stone backrest. These stones not only provide comfortable back support, but also help retain any portion of the soil bank that rises above the finished wall.

First, select a few capstone-sized stones, each with one fairly even surface. In order to match their edges, position them on the ground, setting them on end and bracing them against 5-gallon (19 liter) buckets filled with gravel or stones. When you've found a combination that works, set these backrest stones on the back edges of the wall capstones, leaning them against the soil bank at an angle.

Setting the backrest stones in place

Final Touches

The area just behind the capstones on a retaining wall is a fine one for planting. Cover the visible backfill material with the soil that you set aside when you started and top-dress the soil with mulch. Brush away any loose crushed stone or soil when you're finished. Then take the rest you deserve!

Selecting and matching stones for a bench backrest

Workshop participants enjoying their bench

CRAFTSMANSHIP

On many occasions, you'll find just the right stones for particular places in a wall; they'll almost seem to jump into place. At other times, none of the stones you select will fit, or you'll find the right stone, attempt to trim one edge for a perfect fit, and watch the stone break into several pieces. These are the times when taking a break yourself can turn things around!

It's easy to get excited as you lay a course of stone and watch your wall grow. In the workshops I give, I'm always amazed by how quickly the dozen or so participants work. All that enthusiasm, however, sometimes results in running joints, gravel that hasn't been set thoroughly, or loose face stones. Avoiding these errors is a simple matter of slowing down and paying attention to your craftsmanship.

THE DRY STONE WALLS OF IRELAND

The Irish countryside is covered with thousands of miles of dry-stacked stone walls (or "dry stone walls," as the Irish call them). The tradition of building these walls, which were constructed to mark boundaries, fence in livestock, and clear rocky land for planting, dates back about 5,000 years.

Each wall's style is determined by the stones available, the wall's function, the skills of the mason, and the region in which the wall is located. The two most common kinds of Irish walls are "single stone," which are only one stone thick, and "double stone," which are two stones thick. The single stone wall shown in the photo to the right is located in County Claire, along the west coast of Ireland. The gaps between the stones were deliberately included to allow strong winds to pass through the wall without toppling it. In the bottom right-hand photo, which was taken on one of the Aran Islands, double stone walls follow the contours of the land.

Also taken on one of the Aran Islands, the photo below shows a series of double stone boundary walls made with local carboniferous limestone. These tall walls are stabilized both by their very large foundation stones, which are set securely in the ground, and by their thickness, which is usually about half their height. The walls were built by stacking the double stone courses on top of the foundation stones and filling the voids behind the two faces with smaller stones. Critical tie stones (or "through stones"), which extend from one face to the other, were included in some of the courses to join the two faces together. The walls were completed by "coping" the top with stones set on edge, one after another, along the wall's length.

Today, the same dry stone construction methods are still used to build walls in Ireland. In addition, many Irish communities have recognized the historical significance of the ancient walls in their areas and are making efforts to repair them. 🪨

CHAPTER FIVE

PLANTS AND STONE

*P*lants and stones are natural partners. When they're combined properly, they continue to complement each other season after season. A grouping of stones, whether arranged by Mother Nature herself or by hand, can provide a perfect niche or backdrop for green and colorful growth. Sometimes, plants and stones look so congenial together, it's hard to decide which showed up first.

SELECTING PLANTS

To find out which plants will do best in your region and in rocky environments, visit your local garden center and study a few books and plant catalogues. Of course, the specific location of your stone project will have some bearing on the plants you choose. Ask yourself whether the plants will sit in full sunlight, dense shade, or partial shade. Is the soil well drained or is it usually damp? Is it acid or alkaline? Will the project be exposed to harsh winds or located in a well-protected area? Stonecrops and many alpine plants do fine on windy

Hay-scented ferns, phlox, and rhododendron blend well together.

In some naturalized settings, delicate plants such as these Mexican evening primroses appear to be growing straight from the rocks.

hillsides, whereas tender woodland plants prefer dappled sunlight and a more tranquil setting.

Consider using plants that are native to your area. These will help your wall blend in with the surrounding environment. Be careful to choose varieties that will thrive in the conditions provided by your stonescaping site.

Many nurseries offer native plants. You may also gather them from the wild, but if you do, take only varieties that grow in abundance and leave plenty of healthy plants behind. Also remember to get permission from the landowner if you're gathering on property that is not your own.

You'll find more tips on plant selection in the following sections.

PLANTS AND DRY-STACKED STONE WALLS

The soil in front of and above your retaining wall, whether it's level or sloped, often makes a fine setting for a garden bed. Plants may also be set directly into the wall.

When set along the base of the wall, plants serve as a visual anchor for the stone structure. If planted above the wall or within the upper stone courses, cascading varieties such as trailing cranberries, dianthus, and alpine strawberries will hide some stones while highlighting others.

Some gardeners enjoy the lush and informal look of heavy growth. They select varieties that will drape down luxuriously over the stones and fill the beds above them with eye-catching color. Other gardeners prefer a sparser and more formal look, one that emphasizes the stones rather than the plant growth.

These grey stone surfaces contrast pleasantly with the lush green and vibrant blooms of an Olympic Fire mountain laurel.

Many plants, such as these alpine strawberries, do well in retaining walls.

To set plants directly within a wall, leave a gap between two stones as you're laying a course. This gap must be wide enough to hold the plant's crown (the portion of the plant between its roots and leaves) and a little soil.

The plant should rest on a trail of soil that extends from the interior of the wall back to the soil bank. To prevent this soil from migrating down through the gravel backfill or out through the face of the wall, you may want to start by spreading some landscape fabric over the gravel and over the gap in the wall stones. Cut a hole in the fabric, locating it at the gap; the roots of the plant that you place in the gap will extend through this hole.

The best time to set plants right into the joints of your stone wall or paving project is while you're stacking or laying the stones. This won't work, of course, if you're working when the temperatures are too cold for tender young plants.

Next, make up a mixture of topsoil, composted manure, coarse sand, and water-absorbing granules. (The granules, available at nurseries and garden stores, absorb available moisture and release it gradually into the soil.) You'll need about 3 gallons (11.4 liters) of this soil mixture for each plant you set. Spread about 2 gallons (7.6 liters) over the fabric, from the back of the wall to the soil bank. This trail of planting medium will nurture the plant as its roots reach back for the nutrients and moisture in the soil bank.

Place the plant in the gap, with its crown about 2 inches (5 cm) in from the

When setting a plant in a wall, recess its crown in a gap between two stones and carefully fan out the roots.

Two large chunks of schist rock make a comfortable spot for sitting beneath a northern grey birch, which shades a variety of woodland perennials and colorful annuals.

face of the wall. (Recessing the crown in this manner will protect it from harsh, drying winds.) Insert the plant's crown through the hole in the landscape fabric and carefully fan out the roots on top of the trail of soil. Place another gallon (3.8 liters) of the soil mixture on top of the roots and water the entire area well. Then continue setting more wall stones. The gravel backfill that you add behind sub-sequent courses will bury the soil surrounding the roots of the plants.

Following are a few tips on planting in and around stone walls:

- If your wall sits in full sun, protect the transplants for several days by placing a couple of boards up against the wall at an angle. Draping a piece of burlap down from the top of the wall will also work.

Boulders and stacked stones are the dominant features in this arid southwestern garden.

- Plants set just in front of your wall may receive the extra moisture that drains down through the gravel backfill. Be careful not to overwater them.
- Unless your wall has a full southern exposure, a planting bed at its base is likely to be shady. If your wall does face south, the stones in it will retain heat, so soil temperatures close to the wall will be quite warm.
- If any part of your wall will also serve as a bench, avoid setting plants in areas where dangling legs might damage them.
- Unless you want to see more plants than stones, avoid overplanting. Although young seedlings will look quite sparse during their first season, their foliage will grow significantly during the second and third.
- Small groups of plants, placed in the wall randomly, look more natural than evenly spaced arrangements.

Located in a moist, temperate region, the stones in this winding wall are almost obscured by lush summer growth.

Creeping plants such as Irish moss quickly cover the gaps between stones.

PLANTS AND STONE PAVING

Plants set into the joints of a paved area or around its edges have both practical and aesthetic advantages. By blending stone pavers in with surrounding vegetation, greenery helps soften the visual impact of hard stone surfaces. In addition, plants set within the joints of a patio, walkway, or courtyard help discourage the growth of weeds in these areas by crowding them out. If you select hardy aromatic varieties, you'll also enjoy the marvelous scents they release when they're crushed.

Among the best plants for areas such as paving or steps are creeping varieties that will withstand heavy foot traffic. The leaves of

- Plant varieties that require well-drained soil (alpines and stonecrops are two good examples) do especially well in dry-stacked walls because the gravel backfill guarantees good drainage.

- Woodland plants are happiest in a rich, moist soil. To help retain moisture in their planting medium, be sure to add water-absorbing granules to it.

- Water the plants regularly, especially during their first growing season. The immature roots of young seedlings can't reach back into the soil bank behind the wall, so they'll need your help until they can.

For beds above low retaining walls, choose low-growing plants rather than draping plants that might hide the stones completely.

some—including chamomile, fragrant thymes, winter savory, Corsican mint, and low-growing alpines—will also release fragrant aromas when they're crushed by passing feet. These plants will spread throughout the joints in paved areas and will be kept "pruned" by the people and pets who tread on them.

Usually, pavers are set on gravel beds, and the gaps between them are filled with gravel. As you lay out the pavers, choose a few gaps for planting and instead of filling them, remove the gravel bed from the bottom of each one. Next, mix up some soil, compost, and coarse sand. Then sprinkle some water-absorbing granules in the bottom of the gap. Add some of the soil mixture on top of the granules, set the plant, and add more soil mixture as necessary to fill the gap. (Make sure you place the granules below the soil mixture. I once made the mistake of sprinkling them in the upper layer of soil, and the first heavy rain scattered little granule islands all over the stone patio!)

Water the young seedlings frequently, as the gravel bed beneath the paving will drain moisture away quickly.

Within two or three years, the young woolly thyme seedlings planted in the gaps among these fieldstone pavers will spread profusely.

PLANTERS AND TREE WELLS

*P*lanters and tree wells are simply dry-stacked retaining walls that serve specific functions. The crescent-shaped planters shown on this page were set into existing slopes and filled with layers of lightly tamped soil as the courses of stone were stacked. (Tamping the soil prevents dramatic settling later.) On a level lawn, the walls of a dry-stacked planter should encircle the planting bed completely.

A tree well is a great solution to a problem that often arises during excavation of a building, driveway, or road site. When excavated soil is carelessly mounded around the base of a tree, the tree gradually suffocates. Removing this soil from around the trunk and dry-stacking a tree well to retain the soil at a safe distance can save a tree's life. (Leave plenty of room around the trunk for future growth.)

PLANTS AND STONE STEPS

Plants may be set along the edges of stone steps, between the risers and treads, and within any gaps between stones. Avoid placing large, bushy varieties along the sides of steps, or you'll end up spending more time clearing away the overgrowth than you do setting the stones! For gaps between risers and treads, select hardier varieties, such as fragrant miniature alpine plants and hardy, aromatic "creepers." Tender varieties won't survive foot traffic; they'll do better along the edges.

The thriving sedum set in this flight of steps helps soften the hard-edged appearance of the stones.

Hosta and delicate maidenhair ferns complement the rounded river rocks and carpet of moss in the foreground.

REVEALING A STONE LEDGE

I once spent a day uncovering a large, partly exposed rock ledge for a client. First, I removed some vines and raked away plant debris. Then, with a digging spade and mattock, I removed the topsoil, which I set aside for later use. I also removed all the loose stones around the face of the ledge.

As the work progressed, I used smaller tools. The tapered blade of a brick mason's hammer, a mason's trowel, and a broom helped remove the soil from tight crevices. At this stage, I felt like an archaeologist, unearthing the skeleton of a huge prehistoric creature. By the time I'd finished, what I'd thought was one very large stone turned out to be a series of three linked rock faces that spanned 20 feet (6 m).

After I cleared the stone faces, I combined the saved topsoil with compost and used the mixture to make a bed for bulbs in front of the ledge. Every spring, the ledge serves as a beautiful backdrop for a variety of daffodils and tulips.

NATURALIZING WITH STONE

Single stones or groupings of stones can transform an otherwise ordinary plot into a breathtakingly beautiful landscape. If you're lucky, your property will have large boulders, ledges, or natural stone outcroppings on it already. Often, these are buried, but transforming them into stunning landscape highlights is a simple matter of removing soil from around them and then adding plants.

If your land isn't rich with stone already, a stone yard can provide the rocks you need. Moving and setting boulders requires heavy equipment, of course, so before you spend any money having large stones delivered and arranged, make sure that your own property isn't hiding any. Take a walk around your land, keeping an eye peeled for the occasional rock jutting out of a sloping area or the barely exposed surfaces of rocks buried beneath the soil. With a bit of digging, buried boulders, stone outcroppings, and rock ledges can be brought to daylight.

Once you've revealed part of a buried rock, arranging large or small stones of a similar kind around it can complement this portion of your landscape. You're quite likely to find these additional stones nearby, but if you don't, search at the stone yard for closely matching stones.

It's also possible to assemble a natural-looking outcropping for alpines or other low-growing plants with boulders and stones. A gentle slope is the best site for projects of this kind. If you don't have an existing slope on your property, just make one by building up the soil.

A creative arrangement of colorful plants and huge boulders makes a stunning, naturalized landscape.

This small boulder garden was created by importing and arranging rocks from a stone yard.

To prepare small planting beds in any grouping of rocks, create pockets of topsoil and compost (or soil and scree) on the uphill sides of the stones. These miniature gardens, planted with ground covers or alpines, will enhance the exposed rock surfaces. Add a few dwarf conifers and a simple stone bench to complete the picture. To link an area like this with another part of your landscape, build a stepping-stone path between the two.

The photos on the next page show two portions of a naturalized garden project that was years in the making and that is still evolving. Located at an elevation of 4,000 feet (1219 m), this garden serves as a privacy screen for a house tucked between two other houses on a narrow lot.

Keep these stone arrangements simple and position the stones far enough apart to leave room for plants among them. Use native stones when you can, positioning large slabs with their back surfaces buried in soil or scree (loose rock debris) as if the slabs were part of a naturally developed stratum.

Backfill the areas behind the stones with a mixture of soil and gravel or scree. Adjust the mixture to meet the acidity requirements of the plants you intend to set in it. Your local agricultural extension agent can provide you with information on how to test your soil and make the necessary adjustments.

Given time, plants set among rocks will reduce competition from sprouting weed seeds. Coreopsis and rhododendron complement these large boulders.

The design required the creation of several carefully placed hillocks. These were made by combining packed clay soil and large boulders, and included pockets of amended soil to hold a variety of plants. The hillock shown in the upper photo on this page rises dramatically to 10 feet (3 m) in height.

In the lower photo, weathered stones and evergreens offer year-round beauty while gracefully retaining a low bank of soil. Because many stones in this project were very large and heavy, they had to be set with the help of a tractor. To create a similar project on a smaller scale—one that won't require the use of heavy equipment—just use smaller stones.

Several people created this naturalized garden project, which is located in the mountains of western North Carolina. The moss-covered stones, ferns, and rhododendron all mimic a natural woodland environment.

CHAPTER SIX

PAVING AND PATHS

*P*aved areas and paths encourage us to linger, lounge, and enjoy our natural surroundings. Start with a stepping-stone path or simple paved entryway. Once you've had some practice dry-laying stones, a world of projects awaits you: elegant patios, beautiful courtyards, welcoming walkways, and more.

FIELDSTONE ENTRYWAY AND COURTYARD

THIS PROJECT, AN ENTRYWAY-AND-COURTYARD combination, consists of fieldstone pavers set on a gravel bed. As you can see in these three photos, the entryway portion runs between one exterior wall of a house and a mortared, concrete-block retaining wall faced with stone. I've chosen this as a first project because once you understand how to build it, you'll be able to construct almost any other dry-laid paving project.

Selecting and Defining the Site

A freestanding paved area—one that doesn't sit next to an existing structure—is very easy to build. Paved areas that abut building foundations are a bit more complex and require some careful thought during the planning stages. Why? Because you must make sure that rainwater doesn't drain towards the building or splash up under the building's siding. Unless you grade the site properly, water may damage the

This fieldstone entryway, at Herb Mountain Farm (Weaverville, North Carolina), extends around one corner of a house to form a small courtyard.

siding and flood your basement or crawl space.

To redirect rainwater, most sites next to buildings only need to be graded so that water flows away from the foundation. You'll find out how to do this in just a few minutes. Sites that are difficult to grade properly may require an added drainage system. Installing these can be time consuming, but if you're willing to spend the time rather than switching to another site, use the drainage-system tips provided in this chapter.

Once you've selected a possible site, visualizing the finished paving project is much easier if you lay out its perimeters. For square or rectangular areas, use string lines to define the edges. Pound stakes into the soil at each corner and tie strings from one to another, keeping the strings close to the ground. For more organic shapes, lay out a garden hose or outline the site with sprinkled lines of corn meal. Then familiarize yourself with the results for a few days, making any adjustments you like before you begin work.

Protecting Siding

To prevent rainwater from splashing up from the pavers and touching the siding on the structure, the tops of the stones closest to the building should be at least 6 inches (15 cm) from the bottom of the siding. (Building codes in many areas specify this distance.)

First, remove any sod from the site. Then, to ensure that the ground next to the structure is low enough, make the following calculation:

Average thickness of your fieldstone pavers
+ 4 inches (10 cm) for the gravel bed underneath them
+ 6 inches (15 cm) from the tops of the pavers to the siding

= Required distance between the soil and the bottom of the siding

Now measure the distance between the soil and siding at your site. If this distance isn't equal to or greater than the result of the calculation above, you'll have to remove some soil. Before you do this, read the next section.

If you just can't obtain the necessary clearance, use the following method to protect your siding. Dig a 4-inch-deep, 4-inch-wide trench in the soil next to the foundation and fill the trench with gravel. Rather than setting your paving stones right next to the foundation, you'll set them from the outer edge of this trench.

Determining the "Pitch"

A paving site next to a building must be pitched (or sloped) so that water will run down and away

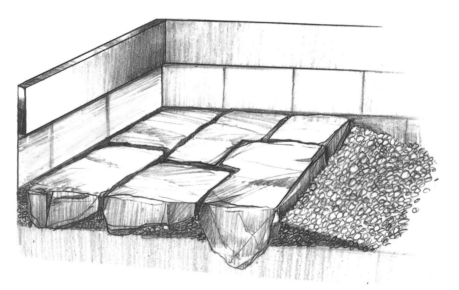

Fieldstone pavers on a gravel bed

from the building foundation. Grading the soil to create this pitch is less critical with freestanding paved areas. If these are located on poorly drained soil, however, they should be pitched to direct water from the site.

The standard pitch for paving projects is at least ⅛ inch (3 mm) per linear foot (30 cm) of paving and never more than ¼ inch (6 mm) per foot. What does this mean? That for every foot of paving, measured from the high point of the site to its low point, the paved surface must slope ⅛ inch downward.

To calculate the overall pitch for your site, first determine the direction in which you'd like rainwater to flow. (Always direct water away from building foundations.) Next, measure the distance from the edge of the site that should be highest (in this case, at the building foundation) to the outermost edge of the site, running your tape measure in the desired direction of water flow.

Now multiply ⅛ by that length. If, for example, your site measures 8 feet (2.4 m) from the building foundation out to the edge, multiply ⅛ by 8. The result, 1 inch (2.5 cm), is the required pitch. The soil at your site must be 1 inch higher at the foundation than it is at the far edge.

Grading the Site

To create the correct pitch at your site, you'll probably need to add or remove soil from some areas. Use a mattock, a shovel with a square blade, and a wheelbarrow to remove soil. To build up the soil, first add a layer of damp subsoil (damp soil is easier to compact), no more than 6 inches (15 cm) thick. Tamp the soil down well, using a commercial, hand-held tamping tool or a homemade substitute.

Repeat this process, adding subsoil in layers, until the desired height is achieved. If your site is 200 square feet (18.6 m²) or more, you may want to rent a gas-operated tamper. Be sure to wear earplugs when using this machine!

Keeping track of the pitch as you grade the site is less critical than monitoring the pitch of the paving stones as you set them, but it's a good idea to check the soil after grading it. Stand at the outermost edge of the site and kneel or lie down so that your eyes are at ground level. From that vantage point, you should be able to see a slight incline all the way up to the building foundation (or to the high point of a freestanding site).

A more accurate way to monitor the pitch is to use a level; a 4-foot-long (1.2 m) model works best. First, set the level on any level surface. Then lift up one end to the proper pitch position. With a 4-foot-long level, for example, lift one end up exactly ½ inch (13 mm); hold a 2-foot-long (61 cm) level up ¼ inch (6 mm). With the level supported in this position, use an indelible marker to mark two lines on the level's vial, one on each side of the air bubble inside it. Then, as you grade the site, periodically rest the level on the ground and adjust the soil until the bubble rests between these two marks. (Make sure when you set your level down on the soil or pavers that it's pointing in the right direction, or you'll end up with a pitch directed towards the foundation instead of away from it!)

Improving Drainage

Good drainage is important, especially in regions that get a lot of rain and snow. When water-logged soil underneath stone pavers freezes, it can cause the soil to heave upward, displacing the pavers as it does.

JAPANESE SURFACE DRAINS

*T*he attractive Japanese surface drain shown in these photos rests in the center of a paved area that extends under and around an open carport. Because the carport was designed without gutters, the drain was positioned to catch water from the roof and carry it away.

To create this drain, the mason wrapped a length of perforated pipe and set it into a trench running directly beneath the drip edge of the carport roof. Next, he covered the pipe with several inches of gravel. To direct water down through the gravel and into the pipe, he then set small stones into the gravel, positioning them on edge and side by side. ⊤⊤

To test the drainage at your site, dig a 2- to 3-foot-deep (61 to 91 cm) hole and fill it with water. If the water hasn't drained away within several hours, the soil in that area doesn't drain well.

If the soil at your site is heavy clay and the site is properly graded, poor drainage shouldn't be a problem. The clay soil will shed water that drains down through the gravel bed, and the pitch of the slope will send this water away. If the soil just beneath the pavers is spongy, however, and rests on compacted subsoil, the spongy soil will absorb water and the subsoil will prevent it from draining downward. One remedy for this problem is to cover the soil with a 2-inch-thick (5 cm) layer of clay soil and top it with a tamped layer of road bond. These compacted layers will help shed water that seeps down through the gravel bed above them.

Drainage problems are also common in two other situations. If the soil at the low edge of a properly pitched site doesn't drain well, water may accumulate in that area. Water will also stand at the low edge of a site if it has nowhere else to flow. The best way to deal with these kinds of problems is to install one or more simple French drains—gravel-filled trenches that are positioned to catch water from the paved area and pitched to carry it away. Sometimes, lengths of perforated plastic pipe, 4 to 6 inches (10 to 15 cm) in diameter, are set at the bottoms of these trenches. (Perforated pipe, which has a solid bottom and slits along its top, is available at home-improvement centers in short lengths that lock together, or in longer rolls.)

Figuring out where to place a drainage system will depend on the nature of your paving project and may require the advice of a landscape architect.

MAINTAINING A PAVED AREA

Even if you've carefully removed every speck of sod from a paving site and have covered the soil with landscape fabric, you may have some unwanted plant growth in the paved area. Airborne seeds have a way of settling into the joints. If you don't enjoy spraying weed-killing chemicals (I don't), keep a vigilant watch for unwanted seedlings and pull them out while they're still young. If you enjoy the informal look that plant growth can lend to paving, consider setting out attractive creeping varieties; these will help crowd out less desirable plants. (See chapter 5 for details.)

As a general rule, the trench should catch water as it flows from the site and should be pitched to carry the water away. Study the graded site carefully to determine the direction of water flow.

To install a perforated-pipe drainage system, start by digging a 12-inch-deep (30 cm) trench, with a pitch of about ¼ inch (6 mm) per foot. Position the trench to catch runoff from the paved area and extend it far enough beyond the site to ensure that it won't release water nearby. Next, to prevent sediment from filling the pipe, wrap it with landscape fabric, tying the fabric in place with string or wire. Place the wrapped pipe in the trench, with its solid half facing down and the perforations facing up. Then fill the trench with gravel.

This two-level patio is paved with quarried stones set in a random design.

Setting Borders around Pitched Sites

Unless the lowest edge of a pitched paving site has a border, the gravel at the outer edge will migrate in the direction of the slope. You may either set your borders before spreading the gravel or, if it isn't critical to you exactly where the borders are situated, you may wait to set them until just before setting the last pavers at the outer edge of the site. Following are some tips on borders:

■ If the ground just beyond the low edge of your site slopes steeply, a low, dry-stacked retaining wall at the edge of the paved area makes an excellent border. Construct the wall so the pavers along the rim of the site also serve as the wall's capstones.

■ Block-shaped chunks of stone make good borders. Sink these stones into the soil at the rim of the paving site and cap them with the outermost pavers or, to add more definition to the rim, choose border stones tall enough to rise above the paved surface. You may need to fill the gaps in the vertical joints by inserting chinking stones, or gravel will leak from between the border stones.

■ Squared timbers, anchored with lengths of rebar, make visually pleasing borders for sites with straight edges. These should be set on 2-inch-thick (5 cm) gravel beds placed along the site's exterior edges, with their upper surfaces just above ground level. The paving stones should meet their interior edges. Start by digging trenches around the site,

(Note that because the ¼-inch-per-foot pitch of the trench and pipe will be greater than the ⅛-inch-per-foot pitch of your graded site, the slope of the trench will be greater than that of the pitched site.)

making them deep enough to hold both the layer of gravel and the timbers. Then drill ½-inch-diameter (13 mm) holes through each timber, spacing the holes 2 to 3 feet (61 to 91 cm) apart. Spread the gravel in the trenches and position the drilled timbers on the gravel. Then drive 2-foot lengths of ½-inch-diameter rebar through each hole and into the ground beneath the layer of gravel. You may either set the lengths of rebar flush with the tops of the timbers, or sink them and plug the holes with wooden plugs.

Setting Borders around Level Sites

Gravel won't migrate from a freestanding paved area that is flat and level, but a border will help define the site visually. If the border material doesn't have too many joints, it will also help discourage surrounding vegetation from creeping into the paved area.

Suitable border materials for level sites include long, squared timbers; lengths of steel edging, ¼ inch (6 mm) thick and 4 inches (10 cm) tall; stone slabs, about 2 inches (5 cm) thick and 8 inches (20 cm) tall, set on their ends; bricks; and Belgian blocks. To prevent borders from acting as obstacles to lawn mowers and feet, set their upper surfaces at or just above ground level.

Spreading the Gravel Bed

After grading the site and setting the borders, spread a 2- to 4-inch-thick gravel bed over the soil. (You may set the borders later if you like.) Consider spreading a layer of landscape fabric over

the soil first and distributing the gravel on top of it. The fabric will prevent any grass from springing up through your pavers.

If your pavers are more than 3 inches (8 cm) thick, spread a 2-inch-thick bed of gravel. If the stones are thinner than 3 inches, spread a 4-inch-thick gravel bed. The gravel will help define the site visually as you work. It will also help keep the site from turning into a mud bath if it rains before you're able to finish the project.

As well as helping water to drain away, the gravel bed makes it easier to adjust the pitch of each paving stone. Even if you live in an arid region, where moisture isn't a problem, it's much easier to adjust pavers that sit on top of gravel than it is to position them properly in soil.

If you choose to use concrete pavers, bricks, cobbles, wood rounds, flagstones—or a combination of paving stones and any of these materials—see pages 93-95 for instructions on adapting this gravel bed.

Rounded river rocks complement a single stone step at the edge of a courtyard paved with fieldstone.

Laying Out the First Pavers

Start placing the paving stones at one end of the foundation. If your paving site meets an inside corner, where two foundation walls or a wall and outdoor steps meet, set the first paver in the 90-degree corner. Finding a stone with a 90-degree corner will be easy at this point because the size of the stone won't matter. If you wait until you've set the surrounding stones, you'll have to search for a corner stone that is just the right size to fit a defined space. (Being this meticulous isn't necessary, but the eye is naturally drawn to corners, and a neat corner will enhance the overall appearance of your work.)

Continue by laying out a row of pavers along the edge of the foundation, leaving ¾- to 1-inch-wide (1.9 to 2.5 cm) gaps between the stones. The edges of these stones don't necessarily need to meet the building foundation. You can always fill any gaps with gravel, rounded river rock, or small pieces of stone.

As you lay out the first few pavers, you may need to add or remove gravel to adjust their heights. Don't forget that the upper surface of each stone must be a minimum of 6 inches (15 cm) below the bottom edge of the siding. Also keep in mind that although the pavers should be pitched away from the foundation, each stone must be level from side to side (parallel to the foundation). Check each one with a level after it's in place. Because fieldstones typically have irregular surfaces, your level will never sit perfectly flat, of course, so hold the level to compensate for bumps and dips on the stone surfaces.

When you've finished laying out the first row of stones, set a straight, 8- to 10-foot-long (2.4 to 3 m)

2 x 4 on its narrow edge, across the stone surfaces and parallel to the foundation. Then kneel down and check to see that the bottom edge of the 2 x 4 meets the stone surfaces as evenly as possible. Pay particular attention to the upper surfaces next to joints between stones. When these surfaces don't meet along the same plane, make adjustments by adding gravel under the low stone while gently prying it up with a pry bar. To lower a high spot, remove gravel from beneath the stone. (Sometimes, stamping on a high stone's edge will settle it.)

Continue laying out stones until you've completed two or three rows, checking each row with the 2 x 4 as you complete it. Also use your level to check the pitch.

Filling Joints

After setting the first few rows of pavers, fill the joints between the stones with gravel. Then settle the gravel by poking it with a metal rod. The goal here is to distribute the gravel evenly underneath the stones. To make sure you're filling all the voids beneath and between the stones, stand on top of each stone as you work, gently shifting your weight from side to side and moving your body around in a complete circle. When a paver rocks as you do this, use your metal rod to rework the gravel until the stone is stable. When you're finished, make sure that none of the gravel remains on the upper surfaces of the pavers.

Use your 2 x 4 and level to recheck the stone surfaces periodically and make height adjustments as necessary. As you continue, if you run into an area that looks perfect for a plant, don't set the gravel in it. Instead, remove all the gravel from that gap. (Instructions for selecting and setting out plants can be found in chapter 5.)

Setting the Remaining Pavers

Before setting the remaining stones, study the photos on the next two pages. They'll provide you with some very useful information. Some of the field-stone pavers shown, which were handpicked during several trips to a stone yard, weigh 200 pounds (91 kg) each. You might want to choose smaller stones for a first project! After we transported these pavers to the building site, we moved them all by hand through a narrow passageway to our small courtyard paving site. We were able to stand some of the squared or rounded stones on edge and "walk" them back to the site. The others we carried (working in teams of two people) or transported in a wheelbarrow.

After setting a few rows of pavers, lay out the stones that abut the borders. This is a good place to set stones with less than perfect surfaces, such as those with tapering edges. (If your site is freestanding and doesn't have borders, set tapered stones with their tapered edges at the outer rim.)

Next, position a long 2 x 4 to span the gap between these perimeter stones and the other pavers to see whether the outer stones are positioned at heights that will ensure a correct pitch for the completed project. Make any necessary adjustments to the outer stones. Then continue setting the remaining pavers, working from the previously paved section out towards the perimeter stones.

If your borders aren't in place yet, set them now and then set the remaining pavers. When all the stones are in place, lie down at the outer edge of the paved area, with your eyes at its surface level, and check the paving for dips or high spots. Also make a final check with your 2 x 4 and level. Fill the remaining joints with gravel and set it well; remember that the gravel mustn't rise above the pavers' surfaces. Sweep any stray gravel back into the joints and hose the surface down to clean it up. Invite some friends over to enjoy the finished project!

FILLING JOINTS WITH OTHER MATERIALS

If coarse gravel isn't visually appealing to you, don't fill the joints completely. Instead, set only a little gravel in each one, leaving an empty channel about 2 inches (5 cm) deep. After you've set all the pavers, fill in these channels with pea gravel, coarse sand, or rock dust. Pea gravel is set in the same way as coarse gravel—with a metal rod. To set sand or rock dust, soak it thoroughly with water. After the soaked material seeps down into the gravel bed, you may need to add more and soak the joints again. Keep these finer materials at least ½ inch (13 mm) below the upper surfaces of the pavers.

If you're working with a combination of stone pavers and thinner paving materials such as bricks, concrete pavers, or faux stones, fill the joints with rock dust or coarse sand rather than gravel.

PAVING

Use a long level to check the pitch from one stone to another. The same tool works well for checking the relative heights of two stones.

To bring one paver closer to another, first remove some of the gravel between them. The tapered end of a brick mason's hammer works well for this purpose.

To move a large paver, jab a pry bar underneath its edge. Then push up and against the bar to move the stone.

A pry bar also helps when you're making minor adjustments to a stone's position.

Use a blacksmith's hammer to break off unwanted protrusions from a fieldstone paver.

Take the time to check the fit of each stone.

Trim away small protrusions that prevent a good fit.

The more care you take fitting the stones, the better the paving will look.

To adjust the height of a thin stone, add gravel beneath it.

Before positioning a large, thick stone, compare its thickness with the thickness of the stones that will surround it.

The wide blade of a mattock makes a good lever when adjusting the height of a large stone.

Some fieldstones can be split in order to reduce their thickness.

You may need to rake away some gravel before setting especially thick stones.

Use a shovel to guide gravel into the joints.

Use the tapered end of a mason's hammer to begin setting the gravel in the joints.

Set the gravel thoroughly by using a metal rod.

A hand broom helps brush gravel into the joints as you work.

FLAGSTONE PATIO

PAVING WITH FLAGSTONE is very similar to paving with fieldstone, but flagstone work has one distinct advantage: It's easier to find flagstones that are close to equal in thickness. It is also relatively simple to cut and trim flagstone to a specific size and shape. Start by removing any sod from the site and grading the area as you would for any paving project.

Setting the Border

For help selecting a border material for a flagstone paving project, refer to pages 86-87. Set the borders after grading the site.

Once set, the border material will define the perimeter of the project and will help retain the bed of gravel underneath it.

Assorted stone sizes, varied "grain" in the stones, and a range of colors make this small flagstone patio an especially attractive spot. Exterior lighting along one edge helps ensure safe nighttime use. The seedlings along the base of the timber wall will eventually fill in this border area.

Spreading the Gravel Bed

Spread a 2-inch-thick (5 cm) layer of gravel over the exposed soil to ensure a mud-free work area. After I spread the gravel for this project, I stood most of the pavers on edge, leaning them against the timber retaining wall to make them easier to scan as I made my selections.

Laying the Pavers

As with any paving project that abuts one or more existing structures, you should work outward from the structures. If one end of your site is enclosed on three sides, start at that end, setting the first stone at an interior corner. Then line up two or three stones on the gravel, next to the corner stone, matching their edges as closely as possible and adjusting their heights by adding or removing gravel.

If your site has an inside corner, always lay out the corner stone first.

Next, working one stone at a time, flip each stone back and, using a trowel, spread a 1½-inch-thick (4 cm) layer of rock dust or coarse sand over the gravel. Reposition the stone on top of this bed, removing or adding rock dust or sand as necessary to adjust its height. To prevent the rock dust or sand from settling into the gravel, some masons add a 2-inch-thick (5 cm) layer of tamped road bond between the gravel bed and the layer of sand or rock dust. If you choose to do this, tamp the gravel down thoroughly before adding the road bond.

Your goal as you continue to lay out the flagstone pavers is to fit the larger stones together as closely as possible. As you do this, you may need to trim one or two small sections off some of the stones and larger sections off others. (See chapter 3 for instructions on trimming flagstone.)

Paving the site section by section is easiest. Arrange several pavers on the gravel bed to cover an area about 5 feet (1.5 m) square, matching their edges and trimming them as necessary. Then, one

Experiment wtih the paving layout by positioning a few stones on the gravel bed.

OUTDOOR LIGHTING

You're just as likely to use a patio or courtyard at night as you are during the day, so consider adding outdoor lighting, especially around areas that are difficult to negotiate in the dark. Lights set near the ground are much more appealing than glaring spotlights positioned in the eaves of a house. They're also much friendlier to creatures such as bats, lunar moths, and a host of nighttime pollinators.

Low-voltage outdoor lighting kits, for use with outdoor outlets, are available for do-it-yourselfers and are very easy to install. (If you don't have an outdoor outlet, consult with an electrician.) The lighting system for this project, which is shown in the photo on page 92, was easy to install and is basically maintenance-free.

Lay out the cable before you spread the gravel bed, placing it on the soil around the site's outer edge or beneath the area to be paved. After grading this project site, I ran the low-voltage cable from the house, across the paving site, and down an 8-inch-wide (20 cm) strip of planting-bed soil that I'd left between the existing timber retaining wall and the paving site. I then covered the short length of cable that crossed the paving site with gravel. After I completed the project, the property owners attached the lights to the exposed length of cable along the retaining wall and then buried that portion of the cable in the strip of soil.

Small stones are especially useful when you need to fill voids between large pavers.

by one, flip these stones back, spread the rock dust or sand beneath them, and lower them back down again, adjusting their heights as you work.

As you lay out the stones, you'll end up with small empty pockets here and there; fill these with smaller stone pavers. Because small pieces of flagstone tend to shift, use heavier, thicker pieces of fieldstone or quarried stone for this job, each about 4 to 6 inches (10 to 15 cm) thick. Alternatively, you may fill these gaps by positioning small, thin stones with flat even edges, vertically. Small pockets are also great locations for colorful stones and ones with interesting shapes.

After setting each stone, use a level to check its pitch. Also check to see that each stone is level from side to side. To check the evenness of the paved surface, set a straight 2 x 4 on its narrow edge, across several stones, and look for gaps between the

After setting each stone on its rock dust bed, check its height and pitch in relation to the pavers around it.

Setting the Gravel and Filling the Joints

After laying out several stones, stand on them as you use your metal rod to set the gravel that's below the layer of finer material. (If you've added a layer of road bond between the gravel and rock dust or sand, skip this step.) Next, rather than filling the joints with gravel, as you might with fieldstone pavers, fill them with rock dust or coarse sand. Flagstone is too thin to stay stable when the joints are filled with gravel; finer materials are required to anchor these stones securely.

Soak the filled joints with water in order to settle the material into the gravel beneath. Repeat, adding and soaking more rock dust or sand until the joints are filled to within ½ inch (13 mm) of the upper surfaces of the pavers. When the pavers have dried, sweep the remaining rock dust or sand into the joints.

pavers and the 2 x 4. To check the pitch over several stones, place a level on top of the 2 x 4 or directly on the stones.

The rock dust that fills these patio joints blends well with the colors of the pavers. The 2 x 4 along one edge helps check the overall evenness of the stones.

SIMPLE STONE PATHS

THE SIMPLEST KIND OF STONE PATH consists of stone pavers set directly into the soil. You won't need fancy tools: just a shovel with a square blade, a mattock, a brick-and-block mason's hammer, and a wheelbarrow. You will need firm, well-drained soil, as pavers placed right into loam or very damp soil will sink. If your soil is spongy, either place each stone on its own bed of gravel or consider making the walkway project shown on page 100 instead.

To make a simple stone path, first outline the site with a garden hose, sprinkled corn meal, or string lines and stakes. A comfortable path width is about 3 feet (91 cm). You don't need to excavate the entire site; just remove the sod.

Start by laying out a few pavers, arranging them in any manner that pleases your eye. Unless the stones are so far apart that someone might trip in the gaps between them, the width of the joints isn't

If your soil is firm and well drained, the easiest way to create a stone path is to set fieldstone pavers directly into the soil.

The slight pitch of this stone path directs water away from a house.

critical. The narrower the joints, however, the less room there will be for unwanted plants to grow.

To match the stones up without leaving large gaps between them, you'll probably need to trim tapered edges from a few. To fill any large gaps that are unavoidable, just plug in smaller pavers, selecting stones that will reach deeply enough into the soil to make them secure and stable.

Once you've arranged a few stones to your satisfaction, dig a hole for each one, flipping the stone back so you can reach the soil. Use a mattock or digging spade to rough-cut the hole; then refine its shape with the tapered blade of a brick-and-block mason's hammer. To compensate for settling, the upper surface of each stone should rise just above ground level. (If your soil isn't firm enough to support the stones, add a bed of gravel to each excavated hole.)

Test-fit each paver in its hole. If the paver's height isn't correct, add or remove soil to raise or lower it. Tamp any added soil down thoroughly (a rubber mallet works well here) before replacing the stone. Use a level to make sure the upper surfaces of the pavers you've set are even. When the stones are at the correct height, fill the joints around them with soil. To stabilize the stones, use your rubber mallet or the blunt end of one of your hammer handles to pack the added soil firmly around the edges. Continue setting stones in this fashion until your path is finished.

Because simple stone paths don't usually have borders, surrounding vegetation will gradually creep into the joints between the pavers. Either trim these invaders while they're small (if you leave them unchecked, they'll eventually cover the pavers) or fill the joints with plants you've selected and set out yourself.

STEPPING-STONE PATHS

THE EASIEST WAY to lay a stepping-stone path (a method that works best in firm, well-drained soil) is to set large stones directly into the ground. (See "Simple Stone Paths" for instructions.) Arrange the stepping stones as you like, but take care to place them so that stepping from one to another is comfortable and safe. Once the stones are in place, pack soil firmly around each one.

The stepping stones shown in the photo at the bottom of the opposite page were set on a base of rock dust, which was spread on top of clay soil. To make a similar path, dig a trench a little wider than the largest stone and spread a 2-inch-thick (5 cm) bed of rock dust in it. Lay out the stones, fill the empty portions of the trench with rock dust, and tamp the rock dust down firmly.

In poorly-drained soil, stepping stones should be set on a gravel bed in an excavated trench and then packed with rock dust or gravel.

Garden beds are made more accessible by a simple stone path.

These stepping stones lead across a creek along a woodland path.

The bed of rock dust under and around these stepping stones stabilizes them. The steel edging material shown in the foreground defines one edge of a wide footpath.

STONE WALKWAYS

THIS WALKWAY DESIGN WORKS WELL in a variety of situations. Its timber borders serve as an attractive visual accent and prevent the surrounding lawn from invading the joints between the rough-quarried stones.

This project is dry-laid in much the same way as the paving projects described earlier in this chapter. The instructions that follow will also work with other paving and border materials, although you'll need to make one important adaptation if you use flagstone or other types of pavers (see page 103).

The walkway shown in this photo is set on well-drained soil, so the site isn't pitched. If your site isn't well drained, refer to the section "Improving Drainage" on page 102 before preparing the site.

Selecting a Border Material

Squared timbers (4 x 4s, 6 x 6s, and 8 x 8s) are among the most common border materials for walkways, but 4 x 6 and 6 x 8 lumber will also work. Large timbers will last longer than smaller ones, and pressure-treated timbers will last the longest. If you don't want to use treated lumber, select a dense, long-lasting hardwood instead. Hardwood lasts longer than untreated softwood, especially if it's set on a gravel bed, and in time, hardwood also weathers to a beautiful, natural color. Unfortunately, hardwood timbers are sometimes difficult to

This project was built by my friend Sammy Cox, who decided to replace the deteriorating concrete path to his front door with a more welcoming walkway.

find. To locate sources, look in your telephone directory under "Sawmills" or "Lumber."

Using lumber of any kind will restrict you to straight-lined walkway designs. To create turns in the walkway, use a chain saw or circular saw to make angled end cuts where timber ends meet. For a more rustic look, use hardwood logs or flat stones set on their edges.

Preparing the Site

You don't need to pitch a walkway site on well-drained soil, but the site shouldn't slope down towards your home or any other structure. Sketch your design on paper first. Then use string lines and stakes, set low to the ground, to lay out the design at your site.

Before you begin, refer to the walkway illustration, which shows two different stages of walkway construction: the excavation of the trench (left) and the placement of the timber borders and gravel bed (right).

Lay out the timbers just inside the string lines and make end cuts as required to create any angled turns. When you're satisfied with the border layout, set the timbers off to the sides of the site. Remove any sod and other vegetation within the string lines.

Depending on the sizes of your timbers and stones, you'll probably have to excavate your trench to two different depths. The portion of the trench directly beneath the paving stones must be deep enough to hold a 4-inch-thick (10 cm) gravel bed and the paving stones set on that bed. The timbers, however, must be set on a shallower, 2-inch-deep (5 cm) gravel bed, and their upper surfaces must be kept just above ground level.

Excavated walkway trench with gravel bed and timbers

To estimate the required depth of the trench beneath the pavers, add 4 inches to the average thickness of your paving stones. To estimate the depth of the trench beneath the squared timbers, add 2 inches to the timber thickness. In most cases, the trench will be deeper beneath the paving stones than it is beneath the timbers.

The next step is to excavate the site. As you dig the trench, if you notice any wet, spongy spots in the soil, pack them firmly with large pieces of gravel or small rubble stones.

Spread out the gravel in the trench. Make sure that the bed is at least 4 inches deep down the center of the trench and 2 inches deep along the edges, where the timbers will be set.

Installing the Timber Border

In each timber, drill a series of ½-inch-diameter (13 mm) holes, spacing them 2 to 3 feet (61 to

91 cm) apart. Next, set two timbers on their gravel beds, opposite to one another and just inside the string lines. Adjust them on top of the gravel so that their upper surfaces are slightly above ground level. If you have a 4-foot-long (1.2 m) level, place it across the timbers to make sure their upper surfaces are even. (If your level is too short to span the gap between the timbers, set a length of 2 x 4 across them and place the level on the 2 x 4.) Repeat these steps to position the other timbers.

To anchor the timbers in place, drive 2-foot-long (61 cm) sections of rebar through the holes. The rebar sections should rest flush with the upper surfaces of the timbers or, if you plan to plug the holes with wood plugs, slightly below them.

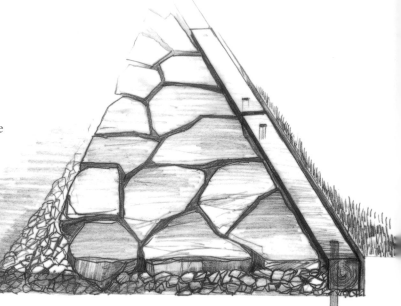

Rough-quarried pavers set in the gravel bed.

Improving Drainage

In poorly-drained soils, it's wise to pitch the portion of the trench directly beneath the paving stones so that water will run down the length of the trench and discharge at the low end. A perforated drainage pipe, positioned in the center of the trench and running down its length, will also help. To prepare the trench for a pipe, dig both sides so they slope down towards the center; these sloped surfaces will help direct water into the perforated pipe. Wrap the pipe in landscape fabric, position it in the trench, and spread the gravel bed over it.

To help correct poor drainage in spongy soils, add a 2-inch-thick (5 cm) bed of packed road bond to the bottom of the pitched trench. The layer of road bond will shed water, while the pitch of the trench will direct the water away from the site.

If your site just can't be pitched and soil drainage is poor, build the walkway above ground instead of setting it at ground level. Use timbers that are 6 to 8 inches (15 to 20 cm) thick, placing them on 2-inch-thick gravel beds just inside the string lines. Then spread a 2- to 4-inch-thick (5 to 10 cm) gravel bed for the pavers right on top of the sod-stripped soil between the timbers. Timber borders placed above ground level tend to look a little stark. Planting dense ground covers and bedding plants along their outer edges will help soften their appearance.

Setting the Pavers

Before setting the pavers, refer to the illustration above. Then review the paving instructions for the

"Fieldstone Entryway and Courtyard" on pages 80-91. You'll set these rough-quarried stones in much the same way. If you choose to use thinner pavers (including flagstone or brick), you must spread a 2-inch-thick (5 cm) bed of coarse sand or rock dust on top of the gravel bed before setting the stones. Although thick stones will be stable when they're set on a gravel bed, thinner stones require a layer of finer material to make them stable.

Start at one end of the walkway, selecting and laying out pavers on the gravel bed and making sure their upper surfaces are even with those of the timbers. Leave 1-inch-wide (2.5 cm) joints between the stones.

After you've laid out all the stones, use gravel (or, if you're working with thin pavers, rock dust or coarse sand) to adjust their heights. Remember that a pry bar or crowbar is the tool of choice for lifting stones. If a stone seems a bit high at one end, either remove gravel from beneath it or stamp on it to settle it.

Using your gravel-setting tool, set the stones as usual, adding gravel (or finer material) when necessary to fill any voids beneath them. To fill the joints, add gravel, rock dust, or sand.

DESIGN TECHNIQUES

*B*y all means experiment with your walkway's surface design. Rather than setting the stones section by section, for example, try laying out large stones in groups of two or three, along the entire walkway, matching the stone edges in each group. Then connect the groups of large stones by filling in with medium-sized and small stones. (When you're creating a narrow paving project such as a walkway, setting the pavers after laying all of them out is easy because you can work from both sides.)

To help water move off paths, many masons "crown" the paving by pitching the stones to slope from the center of the path down towards both edges. The very slight pitch of the stones produces a barely perceptible arc in the center of the path. When crowning a narrow path, be sure to use small stones, as pitching large ones in a limited space is almost impossible.

CHAPTER SEVEN

STONES AND WATER

F or thousands of years, people have devised ways to contain, transport, and use water. This wonderful substance is necessary, of course, but it's also naturally beautiful. The projects in this chapter—a dry-stacked niche for a spigot, practical stone-and-pipe culverts to divert water, and a small waterfall—all make it possible to enjoy the alluring sight and sound of water on your property.

A STONE NICHE FOR A SPIGOT

THIS SPIGOT-AND-STONEWORK PROJECT is set along a woodland path at Winterberry Farm in Haywood County, North Carolina. Its location makes watering woodland seedlings on the farm easy. The stonework serves two functions—one practical and one aesthetic. The stone shelf below the spigot holds a bucket or watering can, and the niche provides an attractive landmark as well.

The stones I had on hand (culls from another project) and the nature of the site itself (secluded, heavily shaded, and rich with plant life) determined the informal, rustic style of the stonework. In a different setting and with different stones, I might have chosen to dry-stack the stones to create a retaining wall within the cut bank, using the shelf as its base.

Preparing the Site

First, you must run a plastic plumbing pipe from a water source to your project site. (If you're not comfortable doing this job yourself, you'll need to hire a plumber.) The trench for the pipe should be 1 to 3 feet (30 to 91 cm) deep, depending on the depth to which the ground freezes.

During the cold months of the year, the water is turned off and the line drained. It's possible to create an all-season spigot by insulating the pipe or using what's known as a "stand-up" pipe instead.

Next, dig a 4-foot-long (1.2 m) and 2½-foot-wide (76 cm) shelf into the bank. To make reaching the spigot easy, the shelf should be rest about 1 foot (30 cm) above path level.

Laying the Stone

Spread a 2-inch-thick (5 cm) bed of gravel over the excavated shelf. Next, set one or two large, flat stones on the gravel. These should cover the shelf and overlap it by about 4 inches (10 cm). Then, position a very large, heavy stone on the back ends of the two shelf stones, tilting it slightly back

towards the bank. Position the end of the pipe on top of this stone, leaving several inches hanging over the edge.

Use large stones to build up the sides of the structure. Then, working from one side of the niche to the other, shape a simple arch by stepping the stones over the vertical stone. Use the edges of these stones to lock the vertical stone in place. Slip the spigot into the end of the pipe and attach it with a stainless-steel clamp.

BUILDING A DRY-LAID STONE CULVERT

A CULVERT IS A DRAINPIPE beneath a road or driveway; it diverts water from one location to another. Culverts catch and redirect water from roadside drainage ditches and prevent flooded roads during heavy storms.

The project shown on the opposite page is a stone retaining structure for the intake end of a culvert pipe that directs water from a ditch along one side of a road to a ditch on the other side. The stones prevent the banks of the ditch from eroding and also improve the area's appearance.

Selecting Stones

Large flat stones set on edge will do the best job of directing water from the ditch into the pipe. Alternatively you may stack stones as you would when building a wall, but be sure to use large block-shaped stones along the bottom course. Smaller stones may be dislodged by the force of moving water.

Preparing the Site

First cut back the sides of the ditch. Make these cuts deep enough to accommodate the stones you'll be using and angle them back about 5 to 10 degrees, so the stones you set against the bank will be battered. The cut at the end of the ditch should be deep enough to hold a large stone, positioned on edge, between the bank and the culvert pipe.

Setting the Stones

Moving water will hit the end wall wth the most force, so use a stone with a large face to cover it. Set this stone on end, leaning it against the bank, with its face contacting the exposed edge of the pipe. Fill any gaps between this stone and the bank with packed soil or gravel. If this first stone doesn't extend to the opposite corner, fill the gap with

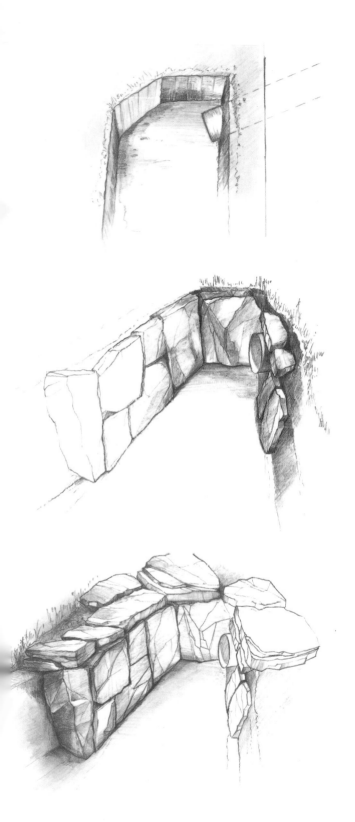

other stones. Then continue setting stones along the bank, working around the corner and down the sides and backfilling with gravel as you go. To cover the bank around the pipe, set a low, short run of stones, either standing them on edge or stacking them. Finally, set large capstones over the upper edges of the stones already in place.

To secure the discharge end of the pipe, just dry-stack a low stone wall around the pipe's opening or stabilize the pipe with large rubble stones.

Annual Maintenance

At least once a year, clean out any accumulated leaves or debris from the base of the stonework surrounding the intake end of the pipe. Lining the bottom of the ditch with rubble will dissipate the force of the rushing water, but I find it much easier to remove debris with a rake and shovel when the soil is bare.

REWORKING A CREEK CULVERT

MANY PROPERTY OWNERS with driveways that cross over creeks or streams already have culvert pipes in place. In this project, you'll learn how to construct dry-stacked walls around the intake end of one of these pipes.

The 4-foot-diameter (1.2 m) culvert shown in the photo above allows a creek to run beneath my driveway. When I first moved to the property, the outflow end of the culvert—a concrete-block wall faced with stone—was still in good shape. The dry-stacked stonework at the inflow end, however, had collapsed into piles of stone on both sides of the pipe's opening, and the slope from the driveway down to the top of the pipe was caving in. The simplest and most practical solution was to stabilize the bank by dismantling the old stonework and restacking the stone walls.

One tip before you start a similar project: Unless the creek or ditch is dry, there's no way to avoid getting wet as you build the stone walls of a culvert! You'll be standing right in the bed of the creek or ditch as you work. To minimize sogginess, wear a pair of tall rubber boots. Making a few walkways by placing boards just above water level will also help.

Dismantling the Old Stonework

I started work when the creek was low. First, I completely dismantled the old stonework on the right-hand side of the inlet end. In order to redirect some of the creek water away from my work area and off to the left, I removed some of the largest stones and placed them in the creek itself.

Some of the original stones were suitable for restacking. The others, irregular in shape, were good backfill material, so I saved them to thicken the new wall and add to its ballast. To supplement the useable recycled stones, I handpicked about ½ ton (508 kg) of stone at a stone yard.

Stacking Flared Wing Walls

During heavy spring rains, the volume of this creek increases dramatically. Sometimes, the water level reaches the bottom edges of the capstones on the right-hand side of the culvert, in front of the hemlock tree. I therefore decided to build dramatically flared new walls—ones that would funnel this rush of water into the pipe. Because the water flow is sometimes extremely heavy, I also knew I'd have to use very large stones.

I dry-stacked the right-hand wall first. I started by wedging stones between the outside surface of the pipe's opening and the soil bank to make sure that water wouldn't flow behind the pipe. Then, to clear a site for the first course of the wall, I removed a few stones that jutted out from the creek bed. Next, I laid out the first course of the wall by placing some of my largest stones directly into the creek.

As I stacked this wall, I set the first stone in each course to overlap the lip of the pipe. I also rounded the wall dramatically in order to make sure that water flowing out of a smaller creek on the right would hit stones rather than soil as it entered the larger creek. To backfill the wall, I combined the irregularly-shaped culls that I'd saved with crushed limestone that I had on hand and small stones gathered from the creek. The creek was also a good source for shims, wedges, and the smaller stones across the top of the pipe.

As I continued to stack courses, I had to remove the lower branches of the hemlock tree in order to provide working space. I took care to leave enough soil and space for the tree's future growth.

After capping off the section of the wall in front of the tree, I cut a shelf in the bank behind the tree and stacked a couple of courses of that wall. Then I shifted my attention to the wall on the left-hand side of the creek.

First, I had to move the water-diverting stones that I'd set in the creek. I placed these at the opposite side to divert water from my new work area at the left-hand side of the culvert. Then I stacked the new wall, using my largest stones in the bottom course and backfilling as before.

The final stage of this project was stacking the wall just beneath the road, which I did in the usual fashion.

WORKING WITH NEW CULVERT PIPE

IF YOU HAVE A SMALL CREEK on your property and would like to install a culvert pipe with a pathway over it, try the following project. If, however, your creek is large and you want to build a driveway over the culvert, I strongly recommend that you consult with a professional. You can certainly dry-stack the stones at the ends of a large culvert, but setting the pipe, gravel, and road bond will require the use of heavy equipment. For smaller projects, you'll only need a pick-up truck to haul the pipe, gravel, and stones.

Culvert pipe is cylindrical in shape and made of rigid plastic or heavy-gauge galvanized steel. Diameters can range from 1 to 10 feet (30 to 305 cm). To create a 6-foot-wide (183 cm) path over a small creek, a pipe 10 feet long and 3 feet (91 cm) or smaller in diameter will be sufficient. To find a local supplier, just look in your telephone book, under "Pipes" or "Culverts."

Have the pipe cut to length before you pick it up or before it's delivered. Most pipe sellers will deliver, but if you don't want to pay for this service, a small truck can usually transport short sections. You can join these with a connector once they're at your site. Elbow sections that allow pipes to be joined at 90- and 45-degree angles are also available.

Determining the diameter of the pipe you'll need is tricky, as there's no way to gauge exactly how much water will flow through the pipe at any given time. One way to estimate the diameter is to observe the volume of water in the creek after a heavy rainfall. Take note of the water's width and depth at the spot where you want to set the cul-

vert; your culvert pipe must be able to cope with that volume of water.

Order a pipe the diameter of which is slightly larger than the diameter you think you need; you never know when the hundred-year flood will hit! If your creek is small and the culvert site is close to its headwaters (where the creek begins), the volume of water may not change drastically from season to season or day to day. If, on the other hand, the site is below a number of tributaries that feed into your creek, or if much new development is taking place upstream, the water can rise dramatically.

Setting the Pipe in Place

Work on this project during a dry season, when the water level in the creek or stream is low. For tips on keeping dry as you work, see page 111.

As you visualize the finished project, keep in mind that the bottom lip of the culvert pipe should sit at or slightly below the bottom of the creek bed. The pipe should slope slightly downward from its intake end to its discharge end.

Start by clearing out any rocks that protrude from the creek bed; set them aside to use in the walls at each end of the pipe. The creek bed must be free of any material that will keep the pipe from sitting evenly along the bottom. Use ¾-inch (2 cm) gravel to fill any holes left by the rocks you remove.

Next, spread a shallow gravel bed down the center of the creek, sloping it downward towards the discharge end and shaping it slightly to match the contour of the bottom of the pipe. The depression in the gravel will ensure good contact between the bed and pipe. Ideally, the lower lip of the pipe should rest at or slightly below the bottom of the creek at the intake end, so don't make the bed too deep.

To position the pipe on the gravel bed, simply roll it into the creek and adjust it by hand. If you're working with two sections of pipe, band them together with a metal collar after placing them on the gravel bed. (Large diameter pipes must be set by heavy equipment.)

After the pipe is in place, stabilize it by placing a few stones along both sides, 1 foot (30 cm) in from each end. Then, towards the center of the pipe, start pouring and tamping layers of gravel in the spaces between the creek banks and the pipe. Your goal is to create a tightly tamped bed that buries most of

A dry-stacked wall made with large stones secures this 9-foot-diameter (2.7 m) culvert at its discharge end.

the pipe and fills the area above it from one side of the creek to the other. Leave enough space at the ends of the pipe to dry-stack walls around the pipe's openings.

WHEN THE CREEK FLOODS

Some friends of mine live in a beautiful valley with a large creek flowing through it. Shortly after moving in, they noticed that during heavy rains, the 4-foot-diameter (1.2 m) culvert beneath their driveway couldn't handle the volume of water in this creek. Excess water flooded the driveway and eroded its edges.

When the culvert was built, it was more than adequate in size, but substantial development upstream had significantly increased the water volume. New rooftops, paved driveways, and other hard surfaces had almost doubled the runoff into the creek. To remedy this situation, my friends widened the creek at their bridge and installed a second, 4-foot-diameter culvert next to the first.

Building the Wing and Head Walls

At the inlet end, you'll build angled wing walls that flare out so they'll funnel water into the pipe. The wall at the discharge end will be perpendicular to the pipe rather than flaring outward. Use the instructions in "Reworking A Creek Culvert" (see pages 110–111) to dry-stack the inlet-end walls first; then stack the wall at the outlet end. As you stack the stones, you'll probably have to add extra gravel behind them to fill the space between their backs and the gravel you poured earlier.

Stack both walls until they're tall enough to ensure that your pathway will be at the height you desire. To stabilize them, add capstones. To make a pathway over the gravel above the culvert, just add a layer of soil, pea gravel, small crushed stone, bark mulch, wood chips, or tamped road bond.

WATERFALL POOLS

WATER—FALLING, TRICKLING, OR STREAMING across stone surfaces and into pools—creates an atmosphere of tranquility and a refuge from the hectic aspects of our lives. Mirror-like pools speak of passing clouds, catch the golden light of late afternoon, and reflect the many moods of each day. Water gardens are filled with enchantment and change in fascinating ways with every season.

Methods for constructing waterfalls and water gardens vary widely. I've chosen to present only one, but if you're interested in others, you'll find many books on the topic at your local bookstore. Landscape designer and gardener Art Garst created all the landscapes shown in this section, with the exception of the waterfall shown on pages 120 and 121. The project described in the following pages— two pools with water descending from one to the other—is shown on page 118. In the sections that follow, you'll find descriptions of the steps Art took as he built this waterfall, but remember as you read them that every site and design will differ. You'll need to study your site carefully and experiment as you set the stones.

Selecting and Preparing the Site

A waterfall project requires a site that is sloped, preferably in a setting that's as natural as possible. As you search for a suitable area, consider the following tips:

- To lengthen a short existing slope, you may be able to build up the area with soil you remove when you excavate a hole for the lower pool.
- To minimize leaf debris, avoid sites beneath or adjacent to large deciduous trees and shrubs.

Falling water splashes over a stone's mossy beard.

■ Creating a pool environment that will discourage excessive algae growth is very important when you're working with water. Algae growth is inhibited by naturally oxygenated falling water and by plants set within the pools. Annual cleaning (see the section entitled "Pool Maintenance" on page 127) also helps. You may add a commercial biological filter to your pool, available from many garden centers, but this isn't essential.

Gathering the Materials

To build a waterfall similar to the one in this project, you'll need some specific materials.

■ The pools shown in the photo on page 118 are lined with EDPM butyl rubber liners. These are usually sold in 10-, 20-, and 30-foot (3, 6, and 9 m) widths at nurseries and home-improvement centers, but can be obtained in almost any size.

■ To hide and protect the liners below water level, you'll use river rocks, as their rounded edges won't puncture the liner. To cover the portion of each liner that rests above water level, fieldstones or rough–quarried stones with two opposing flat surfaces are best, as you must stack them together tightly.

■ A submersible pump moves water from the lower pool to the upper one. Pump sizes vary, depending on how many gallons of water per hour they can handle. The difference in height between your pools will also affect the size you buy. Consult with a pump dealer before making this purchase. The pump that Art used is rated at 1,200 gallons (4,542 liters) per hour, at a rise of about 5 feet (1.5 m).

■ A length of flexible pipe or garden hose runs from the pump in the lower pool to the upper pool.

■ Low-lying areas and sites where the water table is close to the surface are invitations to potential flooding.

■ Placing your pools close to your home, where you can see and hear them, will add to your enjoyment. The pools will also be within easy reach when you need to adjust water levels, check on surrounding plants, or feed the fish.

■ Selecting an upper pool site that is nearly hidden or disguising the site with plants can give the attractive illusion that your waterfall is fed by a creek.

The swirling, recirculated water in the upper pool flows through a channel beneath stacked stones before falling into the larger pool below.

Design Considerations

The size and depth of your pools will depend on several factors. One, of course, is the slope of the site itself. Another is whether or not you want to make a comfortable home for fish. The water in the pools must never freeze solid when the weather turns cold, or your fish won't survive. If you plan to grow water plants, you must also consider the needs of the plants you choose. Some require deep water, while others are happier in shallow pools. The lower

pool in this project is about 2½ feet (76 cm) deep. The upper pool is about 1½ feet (46 cm) deep.

Consider the future position of each pool carefully before excavating the holes. It's easier to create a true waterfall if the bank between the pools is short and steep because the water can be made to descend almost vertically. If the bank is long and only slightly sloped, the water will have to cascade over a series of stepped stones in order to reach the lower pool.

The stone walls lining your pool will be anywhere from 8 to 12 inches (20 to 30 cm) thick. Be sure that the hole you excavate for the pool is large enough, or you'll be disappointed by the pool's finished size.

One warning here: If you don't know whether electrical, plumbing, sewer, or gas lines are buried at your site, check with the utility companies before excavating any soil. Sometimes, these hidden obstacles are easy to move. Your utility company can advise you on this matter.

Preparing the Site

Lay out the circumference of the lower pool first, using garden hoses or sprinkled corn meal. Then remove the vegetation and topsoil from the area inside this line. Also remove vegetation and topsoil from a 1½-foot-wide (46 cm) band outside the marked line. You'll probably disturb the hose line or cornmeal as you do this, so store a mental image of the outline before you start and redefine it when you're finished.

Excavate the topsoil-free area inside the marked line to form a hole that is bowl-shaped at the bottom, with walls that steepen as they rise. As you work, you'll place the soil you remove on top of

A pile of rounded river rocks, ready to be placed on the liner in a pool

These flat fieldstones will cap the rim of the pool.

the 1½-foot wide band to build up a mounded rim around the site. Pick out and discard any sharp-edged stones and large roots from this soil. You don't want sharp objects in it to puncture the liner.

The rim you build at the lower end of the pool should rise about 1 foot (30 cm) above the desired water level. You may need to use quite a bit of the excavated soil to build up the sloped bank that extends up to the site of the pool above. Obviously, because you're working on a slope, the rim will also slope upward towards the back of the pool.

To build the rim, first place a layer of soil about 6 inches (15 cm) deep around the hole. Then pack the soil down with a manually operated tamper, flaring it outward and away from the excavated hole. The rim should round over and slope gradu-ally down on the outside; the mounded soil will stretch over the outer boundary of the sod-stripped band around your site. Continue excavating and building up the rim in this manner, tamping each layer down well, until the hole is the desired depth.

The tamping will prevent later settling of the soil and shifting of the stones.

Next, at the very bottom of the hole, dig another hole a little larger that a 5-gallon (19 liter) bucket. This depression will serve as a sediment catch basin. When you empty the pool to clean it out, the sediment that you hose down from the rocks and liner will be easy to remove from this central location.

Six inches (15 cm) below the water line, on the inside of the hole, cut an 8-inch-wide (20 cm) shelf into the packed soil rim, right around its circumfer-ence. Make sure the shelf is level around its entire circumference by checking it with a string line level (a string with a very small level hooked over it). The soil and liner beneath this shelf will be covered with rounded river rocks; the soil and liner above the shelf will be covered with flatter fieldstones.

The next step is to cut out a 6-inch-wide (15 cm) shelf around the inside wall of the hole, about 18 inches (46 cm) from the bottom. This shelf will serve as a reference point when you cover the rubber liner with rocks and will also help support the rocks. Depending on the pool depth, you may need to add more 6-inch-wide (15 cm) shelves, one for each 18 inches (46 cm) of elevation. The lower pool in this project is fairly deep, and has two.

Protruding sharp-edged objects in the soil, such as rocks and roots, may puncture the pool liner, so you must remove them all. After digging the shelves, check the site very carefully, running your bare hands over the soil to locate these objects and discarding any that you find.

Lining the Lower Pool

The liner for the lower pool must cover the hole's interior and extend about 1½ feet (46 cm) beyond the mounded rim. On the uphill side, the liner should extend to the upper pool site; it will completely overlap the nearest edge of the upper pool. To estimate the size of the liner, measure the pool site at two locations: across its width and along its length.

To measure the width, start at a point 1½ feet from the exterior edge of the rim on one side of the hole. Run your tape measure from that point, over the rim, down into the center of the hole, and up again, to a point 1½ feet out from the rim on the opposite side. (Getting help from a friend will make this job much easier.) The entire length of the tape should make contact with the soil, or your liner will be too small.

To measure the length, start by standing at the low end of the slope, with the excavated hole in front of you. As you take this measurement, your tape will run directly up the slope you're facing.

Stones, water, and plants transform an ordinary slope into an idyllic landscape.

Place the tape 1½ feet (46 cm) out from the exterior edge of the mounded rim. Then run the tape up over the rim, down into the hole, and up the sloped bank behind the hole, until it extends beyond the near edge of the upper pool site.

Ask a friend for help spreading the liner over the hole. Allow the center of the liner to drape down into the hole and place a few rocks on the ends to keep them from sliding back down. Then take off your shoes and slide down into the hole. Starting with the sediment catch basin, gradually work the liner against the walls of the hole, pressing it against the soil as you go. Don't worry if the material forms tucks and folds; these are inevitable. When the liner is in place, temporarily secure its edges by placing large stones on them. (You'll cut the liner to size at a later stage.)

Setting the Stones

Before setting the rounded river rocks, rinse them off well, or clinging soil will add unnecessary sediment to the pool water. Next, place a large flat rock in the bottom of the sediment catch basin and loosely fill the rest of the basin with several large stones.

Start laying out river rocks in the bottom of the lined pool. Select these carefully so they'll fit together closely and cover as much of the liner as possible. The stones must lock together well; unlike stone pavers, they won't be secured by soil or gravel. To settle the rocks, strike each one several times with a 3-pound (1.4 kg) dense rubber mallet.

Continue to set river rocks up the wall of the hole, working until you've lined the first 6-inch-wide (15 cm) shelf with rocks. From this point on, your walls will begin to rise more steeply. You'll use

the shelf as a base for the stones you stack as you continue upwards, but first you must set the pump.

Placing the Pump

The pump should be placed on the side of the pool that is closest to your source of electricity. Attach the hose to the back of the pump and set the pump on the shelf stones. Then construct stone side walls around the pump, allowing the hose to exit from the back, and cap the stone walls off with another stone to form a safe recessed area—one from which you can retrieve the pump easily if it ever needs repairs or replacement. Run the electrical cord out the back of the pump housing, over the lined rim of the hole, to the source of electricity.

Next, run the hose along the shelf towards the rising soil bank. Bring the hose up over the mounded rim and up one side of the bank towards the upper pool. You'll bury it under the stones that you set along the edge of the waterfall.

After laying out the cord and hose, continue to set river rocks right up to the next shelf and then on to the 8-inch-wide (20 cm) shelf above. Use the

River rocks are stacked to the uppermost shelf, which defines the future water line.

largest river rocks available to create the last course; the upper surfaces of these rocks should be even with the shelf.

As shown in the photo to the right, Art sets the stones on the sloped walls of the hole by pulling the liner back over the stones and pounding the soil in behind them. This creates small nodes of soil that press forward, with the liner, to fill the gaps between stones, locking the stones together.

Next, working from the shelf upward, set a few courses of fieldstones or quarried stones with two opposing flat faces, stepping the stones back in each course. The first course of flat stones should rest on the 8-inch-wide (20 cm) shelf and on the upper surfaces of the last course of river rock.

Take care not to crush the garden hose as you continue to set the flat stones in place; weave the

Art compacts the clay soil behind the pond liner by pounding the soil with a mallet.

hose through the gaps and make sure the rocks are secure, or they'll shift.

The rounded river rocks below the uppermost shelf will rest below the water line. The flat fieldstones above them will appear above water level. The hose, shown to the right, will recirculate water to the pool above.

Setting a Runoff Pipe

Heavy rainfall will raise the water level in the lower pool significantly. To prevent the excess water from flooding over the rim, the pool must have an outlet. Before stacking rocks to cover the rim at the low end of the pool, pull the liner back from the mounded soil and dig out a small channel, about 8 inches (20 cm) wide and 8 inches deep. Replace the liner, tucking it into the channel, and position the end of a 4-inch-diameter (10 cm) non-perforated pipe on top of the liner. The open end of the pipe should sit back in the channel rather than hanging out over the pool and should rest at a height that will allow excess water to drain through it.

Now grasp the liner on the inside wall of the pool and tuck it loosely into the open end of the pipe, just around its rim. (You'll have to fold the liner to do this.) Then line the channel walls in front of the pipe with small flat stones, flaring them outward at the end of the channel so they'll funnel excess water into the pipe.

Bury the end of the excess pipe in a trench or simply leave it short and open so that the runoff will flow directly out of the pool and into the soil.

Finishing Up the Lower Pool

Continue dry-stacking stones up to the top of the mounded rim. Next, at the lower end of the pool, use a utility knife to trim the liner back to the rim's outer edge. Bury the remaining liner in the soil at the outer edge of the stonework. Then cover the rest of the rim with dry-stacked stones.

Cover the lined, sloped bank at the uphill end of the pool with dry-stacked stones, weaving the garden hose in behind them, along one side, so you can position it in the upper pool. As you can see in

Flat fieldstones are stacked to form the waterfall area between the two pools.

the photo above, in order to support the waterfall stone, Art placed a very large vertical stone against the lined bank, setting it at a slight angle.

The level shown in the photo below is placed in the half-built spillway, which leads from the site of the upper pool, out to the waterfall stone. Arrange your stones to create a similar channel.

Water from the upper pool will travel through the narrow channel shown under construction here. The electrical cord from the submersible pump appears in the upper left-hand corner. The pump itself is hidden in a carefully stacked stone niche.

A careful stone arrangement sends splashing water into the lower pool.

The way in which you position the stones will determine how the water descends from one pool to the other. A very long, horizontally positioned waterfall stone will direct water out and then straight down; the water won't contact the stones in the bank as it descends. A shorter waterfall stone or one set farther back will allow water to cascade over other stones. After you've tested the flow of water, you'll almost certainly have to reposition some of these stones.

With a bucket of water or a garden hose, check the position of the spillway stones by directing water over them. Adjust the stones as necessary. If your waterfall will cascade over other stones, posi-tion these stones to avoid excessive splashing, as splashing water evaporates quickly.

Creating the Upper Pool

To excavate the upper pool, first pull back the liner that extends up from the lower pool. Then dig a hole, sediment catch basin, and shelves as before and bring the liner back over the front rim of the new hole. Measure and cut a second liner to size and cover the new hole with it, overlapping the first liner as you do.

Bring the pump hose to the uphill side of the second pool and position its outflow end about 1 inch (2.5 cm) below the desired water level. Then cover the liner in and around the upper pool with stacked stones. If your upper pool is considerably smaller than the lower one, use smaller river rocks to line it below the water line.

Pool Maintenance

Check the water levels in your pools frequently and add more water as necessary. You'd be surprised by how quickly water can evaporate, especially during hot, dry weather. Periodically, use a skimming net to scoop leaves from the water and a garden rake to scrape them from the bottom of each pool. To clean the pools, first siphon the water out and hose down the rocks. Then scoop the accumulated sediment and debris from the catch basins and refill the pools with fresh water.

A waterfall garden brings the splendid sight and tranquil sound of falling water close to home.

CHAPTER EIGHT

STEPS, TERRACES, AND BENCHES

*I*f your land is completely flat, you may want to skip right to the section on benches at the end of this chapter. Stone benches make lovely additions to any outdoor setting and although the stones used to build them are heavy, their construction is remarkably easy. If your land includes a sloped area, the first few projects are bound to please you. Dry-laid steps and dry-stacked walls for terraced areas provide practical and attractive ways to prevent erosion, turn slopes into garden beds, and avoid sliding down muddy hillsides on your way to the chicken coop.

DRY-LAID STEPS

STONE STEPS, FORMAL OR INFORMAL, not only serve a practical purpose, but also provide decorative focal points in garden landscapes. Steps and paths should always be your first considerations as you lay out an overall landscape design, so select these sites before establishing sites for walls, garden beds, benches, and stone sculptures.

Treads and Risers

The *tread* of a step is the surface you step on; its depth is the measurement from its front to its back. The *riser* is the vertical front portion. To make sure your steps are easy to negotiate, the depth of the tread and height of the riser (a dimension known as the *rise*) should be consistent from step to step. This

Dry-laid stone steps go hand-in-hand with steep terraced slopes, as they provide easy access to the planting beds behind the terraced walls.

is especially important when the steps are located in a high-use area such as the front entrance of your home. If the rise of one step is 4 inches (10 cm), for example, the rise of every other step should be as close to 4 inches as possible. Why? Consistency in these dimensions creates the sense of predictability that keeps us from stumbling as we go up and down a flight of steps.

The rise of an outdoor step should be between 4 and 8 inches (10 and 20 cm), although free-form steps for private use may be 10 or more inches (25 cm) tall. Tread depths usually range from 10 to 18 inches (25 to 46 cm). The relationship between riser and tread dimensions will vary from one set of steps to another, of course. Steps on a long gradual slope, for example, may have fairly deep treads and fairly short risers, while a steep slope may require narrow treads and tall risers.

Following is one of the best formulas for determining a suitable tread depth and rise:

(Rise x 2) + tread depth = 26 inches (66 cm)

If, for example, you want a 5-inch-tall (13 cm) riser, your tread depth should be 16 inches (41 cm).

Overall Rise and Run

The horizontal distance covered by a series of steps is known as the *run*. This measurement is taken along an imaginary, level, horizontal line. The overall rise of a series of steps is a measurement taken along a plumb, vertical line.

Deciding how many steps you'll need for a given slope requires calculating the rise and run of your sloped site. As you learn how to do this, remember that because stones differ in size and surface area, the dimensions of each step won't always be exact.

The easiest way to measure the rise and run at your own step site is with the help of a friend. You'll need two 2 x 4s, one at least 8 feet (2.4 m) long; a couple of 2- to 4-foot-long (.6 to 1.2 m) levels; a measuring tape; and a pencil.

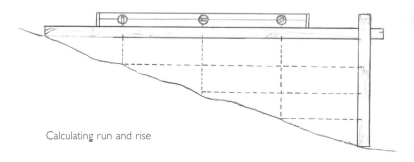

Calculating run and rise

To mark the ground where you'd like the top and bottom steps to be, pound in a stake at each location. Then give your friend a level, a 2 x 4, and the pencil. Have your friend hold the 2 x 4 upright next to the bottom stake, checking it for plumb with the level. Take the other 2 x 4 (the longer one) and position it horizontally, with one end at the upper stake. Check its position with a level as well. The two 2 x 4s should meet at a 90-degree angle. The lower edge of the horizontal 2 x 4 represents the run of the steps; the inner edge of the vertical 2 x 4 represents the rise.

Next, have your friend make a pencil mark on each 2 x 4, at the inside corner where the two pieces of lumber meet. After making these marks, place the 2 x 4s on the ground and measure the marked distance on each one. These two measurements constitute the rise and run of your future steps.

After calculating the rise and run of the slope, you can use the results to come up with tread depths and riser heights to suit your site. For example, if the run of your site is 6 feet (183 cm) and you'd like to have four steps, divide 6 feet by 4 to get the depth of each tread—in this case, 18 inches (46 cm). To calculate the rise of each step, divide the overall rise of the slope by 4; the result is 4 inches (10 cm).

With dry-laid stone steps, it's difficult to keep riser heights and tread depths consistent, but do try to stay within ½-inch (13 mm) of your riser dimension and within 1 inch (2.5 cm) of your estimated tread dimension.

Let me offer two tips here. First, if the run of your step site is exceptionally long, consider incorporating one or more landings. These provide welcome locations for people to stop and catch their breath as they climb. If your steps are narrow, landings also provide "passing" places when someone climbing the steps meets someone on their way down. Landings can consist of small paved areas, level areas of lawn, or border-contained gravel beds. (When you calculate the number of steps you'll need for your slope, just treat the landing as if it were a step.)

Second, a few slopes are just too steep to be suitable for steps. Their run is so short and their rise so tall, that the step treads would be too shallow and the risers too tall to negotiate safely. One way to handle a steep slope is to angle the steps across it; this will increase the run and decrease the rise for each step.

Step Width

The ideal step is 4 to 5 feet (1.2 to 1.5 m) wide and allows two people to walk comfortably side by side. If your steps will serve only as a functional route from one place to another, a more practical width is 2 to 3 feet (61 to 76 cm). Unlike riser

heights and tread depths, the width of each step, from end to end, isn't as critical. This is fortunate, as existing landscape features such as trees sometimes make it impossible to set treads that are equal in width. Consider varying step widths even if other features aren't in the way. A flight of steps that is wide at the bottom and narrow at the top can have a wonderful visual effect.

DRY-LAID STEPS WITH BUILT-UP RISERS

Formal-looking steps have consistent riser heights and tread depths, and the stones that act as treads are supported by separate riser stones.

Selecting Stones

Stones similar to the ones you'd use as capstones for dry-stacked retaining walls, each about 2 to 4 inches (5 to 10 cm) thick, offer good tread surfaces. Look for stones with surfaces that are fairly even and coarse-textured. (Very smooth stones won't provide a good grip when they're wet.) Check these stones for any protrusions on their front edges. If you find any, trim them away, as they may trip people using the steps. If the stones you use as treads aren't equal in thickness, you can make up for the differences by using riser stones of different heights.

Site Preparation

If possible, place your stones at the top of the step site, not at the bottom of the bank. Sliding stones down the bank and into place is much easier than dragging them uphill. Also be sure to have a large tarp on hand for covering the site if it rains. If you want to add lighting along the edges of the steps,

Steps may also be built directly into a wall.

time, setting stones in the cut before excavating for the step above it. If you choose this method, spread a small tarp over each tread after setting it in order to keep it clear of soil as you excavate the next spot. Each time you're ready to move the tarp, slide it off the step it covers and shake any loose soil from it.

Setting the First Tread

At the bottom of the site, excavate a level area a little larger than the bottom of your first tread. (You may set this tread so either its top or bottom surface is at ground level.) Shovel the soil into a wheelbarrow and cart it to a nearby spot. You may need this soil to dress out the site when you're finished.

Next, spread a 2-inch-thick (5 cm) bed of gravel over the level area. Then position one or more stones on the gravel, pitching them slightly downward from back to front to help them shed water. This is a good place to use a stone with a very large surface area, although any tread may be made up of more than one stone. If you use two or more stones, be sure their front edges meet one another as closely as possible at the joint or joints.

Check to see that the upper surfaces are even and that the tread surface is level from side to side.

bring the light fixtures and cables to your site as well. As you set the stones, you'll bury the cables to one side of the steps.

Begin by removing the sod from the entire site. Next, excavate a 4-inch-deep (10 cm) trench, from the top of the site to the bottom. Dig this trench 6 inches (15 cm) wider on each side than your steps will be; this will give you some working space and, if your slope is very steep, will also leave room for the additional stones you must set in order to retain exposed soil. Then make rough cuts for every step, removing the bulk of the soil from each spot where a tread will rest.

Another way to build stone steps is to strip the sod and dig out the areas for the steps one at a

These elegant fieldstone treads were set with and without built-up risers, in order to maintain a consistant rise and run from step to step.

(Humps and depressions in many stones make it difficult to level them exactly, so don't be too picky.) The stones must be secure; treads that wobble are unsafe as well as annoying.

Setting the First Riser

For maximum stability, the riser stone (or stones) for the next step should be placed on the back edge of the tread beneath. If the tread you've set isn't deep enough to allow a riser stone to rest on it, compensate by placing another thick stone behind the tread, one large enough to make up the difference in tread depth as well as support the riser above it. Dig out some soil at the back edge of the tread and add 2 inches (5 cm) of gravel to this area. Then place the additional stone on this bed and pack additional gravel around it.

Riser stones retain the gravel on the step sites behind them and support the treads above them. To figure out how tall a given riser stone must be, first measure the thickness of the tread that will be placed above it. Subtract this tread thickness from the desired rise measurement you selected when you first designed your steps. If, for example, you want the rise of each step to be 8 inches (20 cm), and the tread thickness is 3 inches (8 cm), your riser stone should be 5 inches (13 cm) tall. You may use more than one riser stone to achieve this height; just stack them on top of one another.

Position the riser stone or stones on top of the back edge of the tread stone that you've already set. Then backfill the space between the riser and the soil behind it with gravel. To keep the backfill from

Building up the first riser and backfilling with gravel

WORK YOUR WAY UP

*I*once had a man ask me for advice on building stone steps. He'd already started his project, but was so frustrated he was ready to give up. I started to share some tips on moving the stones and where to start work, when he stopped me, grinning with embarrassment. After a moment, he explained that he'd started building his steps by setting the top one first and was now trying to work his way down.

When you're building steps, always work from the bottom up. Because stone steps usually overlap one another, working downhill is an almost impossible task. Starting at the bottom also provides you with a series of convenient work areas as you move up the slope.

migrating out from behind the riser, you must also set stones at its ends, as if you were creating a corner on a retaining wall. After setting these stones, tamp the gravel backfill, being careful not to shift the stones.

Finishing the Steps

Spread a gravel bed for the next tread. Then brush away all gravel from the top edge of the built-up riser. Set the tread in place; its front end must rest on the riser beneath so that it is well supported. Either set the front edge of the tread flush with the face of the riser or allow it to overlap the riser by up to 1 inch (2.5 cm). If you allow too much over-

In a run of steps, the risers and tread stones can vary considerably in thickness.

hang, the tread will be difficult to stabilize.

Continue setting risers and treads in this fashion until you reach the top of your site. If you're using more than one stone to make up each riser and tread, your steps will be more attractive if you alternate the joints, so they don't fall along a single line from one step to another.

You may find that you need to retain exposed soil along the sides of your steps. On gradual slopes, stand large stones on edge, as shown below, leaning them towards the exposed soil. On steeper slopes, use chunky, irregularly shaped stones.

Adding extra stones along the sides of steps will also provide visual anchors for step corners that jut out sharply from the soil bank. To create a border effect, position these stones so they rise above the upper surfaces of the treads.

Vary the positions of the joints between tread stones from one step to the next and use chunky stones to retain exposed soil.

STONE SLAB STEPS

Formal stone steps may also be built without using any riser stones. Instead, a very thick slab serves as the tread and riser for each step. The front edge of each stone overlaps the back edge of the one beneath it.

Selecting Stones

For this step-building method, use large stones, each as thick as the rise measurement you chose after calculating the overall rise and run of your site. If you want the rise of each step to be 4 inches (10 cm), for example, each stone should be close to 4 inches thick.

Most stones appropriate for this style of step-building weigh in excess of 150 pounds (68 kg). Although the simple engineering tricks provided on pages 38-39 make it possible for one person to move very heavy slabs, unless you can place these stones at the top of your site and slide them downhill as you work, consider making steps with built-up risers and thinner tread stones instead.

If your site is steep, the stones may need to be as thick as 8 inches (20 cm) and may be relatively short from front to back. Your goal, as you construct these steps, is to keep variations in rise and tread depth to within ½ inch (13 mm) and 1 inch (2.5 cm) respectively. If your stones vary in thickness, add shim stones as needed. You don't need to make every finished tread the same width from one side to the other. Instead, use plants or chunky stones to fill any gaps at the ends.

Setting the First Stone

Select the stone or stones for the first step. If you use several stones to make this first tread, be sure their meeting edges match well.

Slide the stone or stones down to the base of the site. Excavate an area for the first step, making it slightly larger than the surface area of the stone or stones. Spreading a 2-inch-thick (5 cm) bed of gravel is optional with very large stones; their weight will prevent them from shifting. A gravel

The consistent thickness of these carefully selected stone slabs eliminated the need for built-up risers.

Located at the North Carolina Arboretum in Asheville, North Carolina, these steps include shim stones to keep the rise consistent from step to step.

base, however, does make minor adjustments easier.

Set the first stone or stones in place, pitching the step slightly downward from back to front and checking it for level from side to side. Then use a metal rod to pack gravel around its edges or, if you're using rock dust or soil, a rubber mallet. To retain the soil along the outer edges, set chunks of stone as needed.

Spread a small tarp across the step you've just set and prepare a level site for the second step, right behind the first one. Before you excavate the soil from the bank, select a stone for this step and measure its depth so you don't cut too far back into the bank. If you want this next step to sit on a bed of gravel, dig this area 2 inches (5 cm) deeper than the upper surface of the first step and then spread out the gravel bed. If

Stonemason Frederica Lashley selected large stones with wide, even surfaces so that the steps she built would be easy to negotiate in spite of their variations in height.

you've decided to set your stones without gravel beds, excavate this spot to make the soil level with the upper surface of the first step.

Because the second step will overlap the first one, you must also mark the first tread where you want the front edge of the second step to sit. Use a tape measure to measure off the desired tread depth on the first step (18 inches or 46 cm, for example),

running the tape back from its front edge. Then make a mark by scoring a light line with a chisel. Set the stone or stones for the second step by placing the front edge of each stone at the marked line.

Check the second step for level and pitch; then continue setting stones until the steps have been completed.

FREE-FORM STEPS

The free-form steps described in this section are the easiest and quickest stone steps to build because you can use a wide variety of stones rather than carefully selected stone slabs. You must use large, heavy stones, but they don't need to be perfectly shaped; climbing informal free-form steps can sometimes be almost like climbing boulders! You may also incorporate other materials, such as short logs.

The steps shown in the photo on this page extend down a steep bank, at the base of which are a creek and small dam. The dam serves as the water intake for a small micro-hydroelectric unit, so silt from the creek must be removed from the dam from time to time. The silt is shoveled into perforated containers, allowed to drain, and then carried up the bank and used as a garden soil amendment. Before I built these steps, the damp, bare, shady bank was quite difficult to negotiate. Fortunately, I was able to place my materials at the top of this site, so I didn't have to drag the stones up the bank as I worked.

When I designed these steps, function was my primary consideration, as the site isn't very visible, and the steps aren't used by the general public. The steep, short bank required unusually tall risers. None of the risers or treads are the same size.

As you can see in the photo, the first step is supported by the dam and by small stones that I pulled from the creek and placed to one side of the dam. The illustrations on the opposite page show the various stages of building these steps. (Note that the dam doesn't appear in these illustrations.)

First, I made the cuts in the bank with a short-handled digging spade. Because my stones were so large and heavy, I didn't need to

Free-form steps can be as beautiful as they are functional.

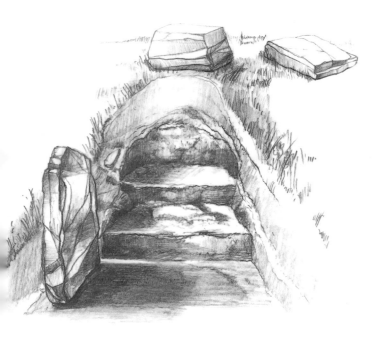

spread gravel beds for them, but if you use smaller stones, be sure to set them in gravel. I slid the first stone down the bank, leaving the remaining stones at the top and out of the way.

After setting the first stone securely, I rolled a large, block-shaped stone into place to serve as the next tread. Then, to prevent the exposed soil at its ends from spreading across the surfaces of the steps, I set irregularly shaped, chunky stones in place along the edges.

The third step required some shimming along its front edge. To support the front edge of the last stone, I placed a long stone on its narrow edge, sinking that edge 4 inches (10 cm) deep in the ground.

Set in a remote area of Grandfather Mountain, in North Carolina, these free-form stone steps were made with large stones found nearby.

LOCUST-LOG-AND-STONE STEPS

*I*built the serpentine steps shown here with a combination of large stones and locust logs. Because I didn't have any help on this project, I relied heavily on my pry bar, a few wide locust boards, and the force of gravity.

At the top of the slope, I was able to unload enough stones from my truck to build the upper three-quarters of the steps. One by one, I slid the huge stones to the edge of the tailgate and then flipped them over onto the ground. (A bed liner in the back of your truck will make this job infinitely easier.) After each stone hit the ground, I moved it off to one side, so the next stone wouldn't land on top of it.

To build the first few steps, I used locust logs, placing each one on a bed of gravel. To stabilize the logs, I pounded large locust stakes into the soil in front of them. To create the flat tread area on each log, I used a chain saw to cut a series of kerfs and then removed the excess wood with a hammer and chisel.

I chose a stone for the next step and excavated a place for it. To move the stone down from the top of the site, I arranged wide locust boards end to end, down the bank, to a point just above the locust-log steps. Next, I walked the stone, on its edges, over to the top board. I set the stone down flat on the board and slid it halfway down. Then I moved to the downhill side of the stone and supported it while tugging and sliding it down over the boards. (At times, I had to hold the stone back to keep it from moving down the boards too quickly.)

To distribute the weight of extremely thick stones, I placed another board next to the one already in place to provide extra support. When the stone I was moving reached the bottom end of the paired boards, I moved the extra board and placed it by the next board down. Sometimes, a stone would start to shift off the two boards; I used a pry bar to shove it back into place. ▄▄

RETAINING WALLS FOR TERRACES

FOR CENTURIES, PEOPLE AROUND THE WORLD, from Italy to Asia and South America, have cut terraces into sloped land and buttressed the soil banks with dry-stacked retaining walls. These walls transformed steep slopes into arable land, protected hillside towns and temples, and even served as seats in amphitheaters.

In today's gardens, terraced walls are usually built to provide level areas for planting and to make

Rising up from the Mediterranean coast, these terraced walls were built 8 to 10 feet (2.4 to 3 m) tall in order to provide strips of level soil 4 to 5 feet (1.2 to 1.5 m) wide.

steep slopes more accessible and attractive. Separating a slope into narrow terraces by building several short retaining walls, one above the other, offers a more attractive result than building very tall retaining walls with huge stones. Low stone walls are also much easier to stack; lifting large stones above shoulder height or working from scaffolding is difficult!

Creative combinations of materials such as locust logs and stones can provide wonderful effects. I've even seen a terrace supported by an 8-foot-tall (2.4 m) retaining wall made with used tires—and the wall looked charming! The over-lapped tires were stepped gradually back into the bank behind them; the exposed holes in them were filled with soil and planted with wildflowers. Large slabs of recycled concrete walkway also make good dry-stacking material. Treated landscape timbers and railroad ties are practical choices, but walls built with them often lack visual appeal.

Depending on how steep your site is, and the visual impact you wish to make, terraced retaining

Built with stone, gravel, and soil, these terraced walls along the Cinque Terra of northern Italy are more than seven centuries old.

The soil behind terraced walls doesn't have to be perfectly level. These slightly sloped beds are perfect for planting.

walls can take any number of shapes. The photos in this section depict just a few of the many design possibilities.

Before sketching your terrace design or excavating the site, calculate the rise and run of the slope, using the method described on page 131. (If you have access to a surveyor's transit and know how to use it, by all means do!) Then figure out the location of each retaining wall as if the wall itself were a step riser and the bed behind it were a tread.

Always start at the bottom of the slope. If you're having stones delivered from a stone yard, ask the driver to leave only enough stone there to build the first wall. Set the remaining stones at the top of the slope. If you can't get your materials to the top of the site, enlist some friends or hire someone to help.

My neighbor Jackie Taylor combined stones and locust logs to create garden beds in her backyard.

STONE BENCHES

IMAGINE TAKING A WELCOME REST and enjoying your favorite vista while you sit on a bench you've built yourself. A well-built stone bench, set in a favorite location, will see years of use and will require little or no maintenance.

FREESTANDING BENCHES

Freestanding benches—the simplest kind to build— may be located almost anywhere: under a tree, in the middle of a garden, on a woodland path, or next to a playground.

Although stone benches may not be as comfortable as garden furniture, when they're set in the right location, they're just as inviting. Choose a site to

The oddly shaped supports of this playful-looking bench nevertheless provide a stable base for the bench stone.

which you've always been drawn. A bench set in an area that you rarely visit won't get the use it deserves.

The size of your bench stone (the stone you'll sit on) will determine how difficult it is to set.

This massive stone slab conceals the supporting stones, giving the impression that the bench is floating.

Some of the benches shown in this section were built by a single person, but help from a friend always makes setting these heavy stones easier.

I keep an eye out for bench stones every time I visit the stone yard. Good bench stones vary in size, but should be at least 3 to 5 feet (91 to 125 cm) long. Positioning a stone this size is a manageable task for one or two people, unless the stone is exceptionally thick. Look for a large slab with an even and fairly level top. An even bottom will allow the supporting stones to make good contact.

A cornerstone from an abandoned foundation was used to make this stunning bench.

One way to support a bench stone is to place two substantial stones underneath it. As you calculate the required height of these two stones, keep three facts in mind. First, a comfortable height for the upper surface of a bench is 16 to 18 inches (41 to 46 cm). Second, you'll set the two supporting stones about 4 to 6 inches (10 to 15 cm) deep in the soil—and even deeper if they're especially narrow. Third, you must include the thickness of the bench stone as you estimate the overall height of the bench.

Let's consider an example. You've decided that you want your bench to be 17 inches (43 cm) tall. Your bench stone is 4 inches thick, so you subtract 4 inches from 17 inches to get 13 inches (33 cm). Your supporting stones will be set 5 inches (13 cm) deep in the ground, so you add 5 inches to 13 inches. The height of each supporting stone should therefore be 18 inches (46 cm).

Look for supporting stones that are close to equal in height. (You may compensate for minor differences by sinking the taller stone further into the ground.) The tops should be fairly flat and even, so they'll make good contact with the bench stone, and the bottoms must sit securely in the soil.

When you're ready to build the bench, start by measuring the length of the bench stone. Next, set the supporting stones so the bench stone will overlap them by 6 to 8 inches (15 to 20 cm) at each end. Make sure the tops of the supporting stones are level. Then set the bench stone. If this stone is heavier at one end than at the other, allowing the lighter end to overlap its supporting stone by a greater length makes the bench appear more balanced.

Another way to support a bench stone is to stack stones horizontally beneath it. If the ground is firm, dig a shallow, level spot for the first stone. In soft, loamy soil, excavate an area large enough to

This simple stone bench is a great place to greet the morning sun.

Whether you're working alone or have the help of a friend, take care to adjust this stone carefully on its supports. To find the best possible position, you may need to slide the bench stone back and forth across the supports until it's stable.

Retaining Wall Benches

A bench may also be built right into a dry-stacked retaining wall. The portion of the wall that serves as the bench should be 16 to 18 inches (41 to 46 cm) in height. The simplest way to build a backrest for this kind of bench is to set large stones on edge, leaning them back against the soil bank at any angle that's comfortable for you.

A backrest may also be dry-stacked as a part of the retaining wall. To do this, you must cut back into the soil bank in order to accommodate the

hold both the first stone and a 4-inch-thick (10 cm) bed of gravel underneath it. Tamp the gravel into the excavated area, set the first stone, and tamp more gravel around it. Check the stone for level; then continue dry-stacking stones to build the support. Two to three large stones look better in these kinds of supports than several smaller stones. Try to use large stones that fit together tightly. If you need to use smaller chinking or shim stones to steady the bench stone, place them in the least visible areas. A bench stone that rocks even slightly is very bothersome.

Climbing vines lend old-world charm to this dry-stacked bench.

A single stone serves as a backrest for this retaining-wall bench.

backrest stones. You must also tie the backrest stones into the wall stones at the back corners of the bench and set capstones at its top. Whether you stack them as part of the wall or set them separately, backrest stones should rest on the back edges of the bench stones, about 18 inches (46 cm) from the front of the bench.

The bench at the corner of this wall includes a raised ledge that makes a fine armrest.

CHAPTER NINE

STONE EXPRESSIONS

E *very time we dry-stack a wall or build a*
stone sculpture, we join the thousands of
people before us who have expressed them-
selves in stone. Magnificent Incan temples, humble
Viking hearths, Egyptian pyramids, Stone-Age Druid
burial sites, and simple stone walls in pastures all
give voice to an essential aspect of our lives: our need
for shelter, for permanence, for spirituality, and for
beauty.

A Stone is Not a Rock

A stone is not a rock.
For a billion years
the trees have laughed at the wind.
And the sea changed rock into aging sand.

Into the night
the doors of the mountain swing.
Into the saloons of morning.
Where we see ourselves in flowers
and in the voice of wilderness that sings.

Someday we will be
what we have always been:
stones in the pregnant bellies of larger rock.
Waiting for birth.
Waiting for the one who
places us gently
into the perfect wave of the wall.

Somewhere in the eye of this rock
    which is often home,
there is a place that is built for sleep.
A kind of haven from the lack of light.
A sort of silence from the sound of pain,
Near beginnings.
Not far from that which ends.
The eye of the day. Or the sky of memory
in the ocean's blood.
Where after work
I wash my hands with the dew.
Searching for boundaries in the answers
to questions I will someday love.

Thomas Rain Crowe

THIS STONE CAIRN, which I dry-stacked over a period of several weeks, was inspired by the need to make something nonfunctional. Whenever I had a free hour at the end of a day, I unwound by working on this satisfying expression of my appreciation for stone. The rhododendron blooms had vanished before I finished, but the stonework still reflects the seasons. As I write this paragraph, the sculpture is dusted with snow.

Jerry Worley, a local farmer and friend of mine, helped me find the stones; all of them came from his pasture. Jerry also helped me set the very large pedestal stone. Once the pedestal was in place, I decided to stack small, thin stones tightly on top of it to form a central column. To stabilize these stones, I set gravel in the center. Then I made a platform, stepping the stones out slightly to create a spiraling effect. For extra support under portions of the spiral, I inserted wedge stones.

My neighbor Greg Ford stacked this whimsical stone piece. In spite of its precarious appearance, the sculpture has proven to be surprisingly stable.

Stone often lends itself to simple designs. This sandstone table, made with only two stones, adds a true touch of elegance to the patio of a southwestern home.

With its perfectly centered lichen medallion, this triangular piece of quartz gneiss stone makes a beautiful garden ornament.

Function and beauty join hands in this artistic arrangement. The flat stone is a canvas for delicate shadows and a perch for resident frogs and migrating birds.

The ruins of Ollantay tambo (or town) are located about 1 mile (1.6 km) from Machu Picchu, in the Andes mountains of Peru. The extraordinary stonework of the ancient Incan people who built these structures is world renowned.

The stones in the wall shown to the right, located in Machu Picchu, were cut to a near-perfect interlocking fit.

Because the ground was so rocky, the Stone-Age Druids of Ireland buried their dead above ground, in chambers known as "dolmens." Each dolmen consisted of a capstone supported by upright stones, which were probably covered by a mound of soil or surrounded by soil walls that left the capstone and entry portal exposed. Poulnabrone (or "the hole of sorrows") is a famous dolmen located in "The Burren," County Claire, Ireland.

The Standing Stones of Stenness (Orkney, Scotland) once formed a late Neolithic circle that may have been a site for worship and sacrifice. Only a few of the original ten to twelve stones remain standing.

Avebury—a prehistoric Druid site not far from Stonehenge—dates back to the late Neolithic period—about 2500 to 2000 B.C. The huge circle of about 100 standing stones enclosed two smaller stone circles. Probably a ceremonial site, Avebury was reconstructed during the 1930s. At one time, it may have been more impressive than Stonehenge itself.

ACKNOWLEDGMENTS

I'm very grateful to the many people who gave so generously of their knowledge and time in support of this publication. I sincerely hope that the stonemasons (some of them unknown) whose work is represented in this book will not go unnoticed, as they have contributed to a remarkable tradition.

My special thanks go to

Celia Naranjo

' Robbie Oates, stonemason (Gardensphere, P.O. Box 4, Sugar Grove, NC 28679), for writing the section in chapter 3 entitled "Trimming Stones for Walls," for his technical assistance and collaboration on many sections of this book, and for his help with location photography. Examples of Robbie's stonework are shown on pages 26, 40, 55, 72, 128, 134, and 137.

' Art Garst, landscape designer (Landscape Gardeners, a design/build company, 7 Buena Vista Rd., Biltmore Forest, NC 28803), for his technical assistance and collaboration on the section in chapter 7 entitled "Waterfall Pools" and for his help with location photography. Some photos of Art's work appear on pages 96, 115, 117, 122, 126, 127, 130, and the front cover.

' Chip Smith, soil scientist (Natural Resources Conservation Service, USDA, Asheville, NC), for his technical assistance with chapter 2, "Stone and Gravel."

' Frederica Lashley, stonemason (The Unturned Stone, Asheville, NC), for her help with location photography. Examples of Frederica's stonework are shown on pages 49 and 139.

' Lowell Hayes, artist and landscape designer (Hard To Find art gallery, Valle Crucis, NC), for his technical assistance on the section in chapter 5 entitled "Naturalizing with Stone." Examples of Lowell's designs are shown on pages 28 and 84.

' Jim MacMillan, stonemason (Fine Stone Work, Boone, NC), for technical assistance with the sections on paving with stone. Examples of Jim's craftsmanship are shown on pages 78 and 84.

Thanks to the following people, all of whom contributed photos to accompany those taken by Evan Bracken (Light Reflections, Hendersonville, NC):

' Richard Babb, photographer (Asheville, NC), pages 38 (top), 90, and 91
' Thomas Rain Crowe, poet and publisher (New Native Press, Cullowhee, NC), pages 1, 3, 61 (top), 156, and 156-57 (bottom)
' Bernie K. Digman, photographer (Las Cruces, NM), pages 4 (left), 21, 23, 42, 43, 68 (top), 71 (bottom left), and 154 (top right)
' William R. Laity, landscaping/construction (Asheville, NC), pages 144 (bottom) and 144-45 (top center)
' Leah Leitson, studio potter (Asheville, NC), page 155 (bottom)
' Celia Naranjo, art director (Lark Books, Asheville, NC), pages 99 (top) and 153 (bottom left and right)
' Ruth Smith, educator (Santa Cruz, CA), page 155 (top)
' Martin Thies, photographer (Asheville, NC), pages 60, 61 (bottom), and 157 (top)
' Susan Wright, garden designer (Shady Grove Gardens, Vilas, NC), page 134

For their help with location photography, thanks to

Donna Billings and Dennis White, Asheville, NC
Chrissie Callejas, Sugar Grove, NC
Judy Carter and Susan Sluyter, Wintersun Farm (B & B), Fairview, NC
Marge and Mac Cates, Linville, NC
Marshall and Elizabeth Chapman, Linville, NC
Sammy and Candace Cox, 4-H Camp, Swannanoa, NC
Jake and Florence Haynes, Linville, NC
Herb Mountain Farm, Weaverville, NC
Peggy Irving, Linville, NC
Lilly Whites Stone Company, Farming, NM
Dick McDonald and Kate Cahow, Sugar Grove, NC
Dr. Tom Milton and Ellen Williams, Biltmore, NC
The North Carolina Arboretum, Asheville, NC
Laurie and Robbie Oates, Sugar Grove, NC
Bud Poe and Rebecca Digman, Placitas, NM
Dr. Rodney and Laura Pugh, Biltmore, NC

Stills Stone Company, Fairview, NC
Jackie Taylor, Haywood County, NC
Bob and Lillian Turchin, Hound Ears, NC
Tom and Sheila Williams, Waynesville, NC
Winterberry Farm, Haywood County, NC

Special thanks also to my parents, Philip and Ann Reed, for their encouragement, enthusiasm, and support; Jackie Taylor, my friend and neighbor, for her creative advice and the loan of her camera equipment; Thomas Rain Crowe, for his photos and permission to publish his poem (page 152); the staff at the North Carolina Arboretum and the workshop participants present on the day of the photo shoot; and Scott Lowery, for his beautiful illustrations.

My thanks to Rob Pulleyn, publisher (Lark Books, Asheville, NC), for his appreciation of stone, for his goodwill, and for cheerfully consenting to publish *The Art & Craft of Stonescaping*; Chris Rich, my editor at Lark, for her concise editing, creative problem-solving, and fine craftsmanship; and Evan Bracken, for his excellent photography and his ability to conjure up clouds when necessary.

Finally, thanks to Celia Naranjo, the book's superb art director and my beloved friend, whose valued professional advice and personal encouragement helped immensely in shaping this book.

The author's photos appear on pages 8, 12 (top right), 13 (top and center), 15 (right), 16 (bottom), 17, 20, 27, 29, 30, 32, 35, 36, 41, 44, 45 (center and bottom), 46 (top left), 48, 49, 53, 63 (right), 66, 70, 71 (bottom right), 78, 79, 80, 81, 84 (bottom left and right), 87, 92, 93, 94, 95, 109, 118, 119, 123, 124, 129, 133, 136, 139, 140, 142, 146 (top), 148, 150, 153 (top and center), and 154 (top left and bottom left). Photos of his stonework are shown on pages 31, 44, 58-59, 80-81, 92, 143, 147, and 148.

METRIC CONVERSIONS

Inches	CM	Inches	CM
1/8	0.3	30	76.2
1/4	0.6	31	78.7
3/8	1.0	32	81.3
1/2	1.3	33	83.8
5/8	1.6	34	86.4
3/4	1.9	35	88.9
7/8	2.2	36	91.4
1	2.5	37	94.0
1 1/4	3.2	38	96.5
1 1/2	3.8	39	99.1
1 3/4	4.4	40	101.6
2	5.1	41	104.1
2 1/2	6.4	42	106.7
3	7.6	43	109.2
3 1/2	8.9	44	111.8
4	10.2	45	114.3
4 1/2	11.4	46	116.8
5	12.7	47	119.4
6	15.2	48	121.9
7	17.8	49	124.5
8	20.3	50	127.0
9	22.9		
10	25.4		
11	27.9		
12	30.5		
13	33.0		
14	35.6		
15	38.1		
16	40.6		
17	43.2		
18	45.7		
19	48.3		
20	50.8		
21	53.3		
22	55.9		
23	58.4		
24	61.0		
25	63.5		
26	66.0		
27	68.6		
28	71.1		
29	73.7		

1 square inch	6.452 cm²
1 square foot	.093 m²
1 square yard	.836 m²
1 cubic inch	16.387 cm³
1 cubic foot	.028 m³
1 cubic yard	.765 m³

Volume

1 gallon (128 fl. oz.)	3.785 liters

Weights

1 pound	.454 kilograms
1 ton	1017 kilograms

Temperatures

To convert Fahrenheit to Centigrade (Celsius), subtract 32, multiply by 5, and divide by 9.

To convert Centigrade (Celsius) to Fahrenheit, multiply by 9, divide by 5, and add 32.

INDEX